THE
SURPRISE
RESTAURANT
MANAGER

www.korgenhospitality.com

ISBN: 978-1-7-362823-0-4 (print)
ISBN: 978-1-7-362823-1-1 (ebook)

Ordering Information:
Special discounts are available on quantity purchases by corporations, associations, and others. For details, contact info@korgenhospitality.com

To the cofounder of Korgen Hospitality, my amazing wife, Morgen. I never would have completed this book without your love and support. You are the best surprise in my entire life.

THE
SURPRISE
RESTAURANT
MANAGER

KEN MCGARRIE

FOREWORD BY FABIO VIVIANI

CONTENTS

FOREWORD

BY FABIO VIVIANI

Introduced to US audiences for his participation on two seasons on Bravo's Top Chef, *celebrity chef Fabio Viviani has since opened 40+ incredibly successful restaurants nationwide, authored four best-selling cookbooks, and hosts the popular YouTube series "Fabio's Kitchen."*

Before I even begin any part of this foreword, I'd like to make a point about what being a restaurateur feels like. With a company that encompasses over 40 hospitality concepts in nearly a dozen different states—from hotels to gaming facilities to stand-alone restaurants to bars and quick service, as well as fast casual and event venues—my team and I basically have our hands in anything and everything that has to do with people eating, drinking, lodging, and having fun. So now let's chat for a second about what our business is really like.

The best way I can describe this business is that it feels like a consistently unexpected sucker punch in the face.

I'm not talking about a "you are fighting with someone and all of sudden you get punched in the face" type of feeling. I'm talking about you're minding your own business, enjoying the scenery and the people around you, and then BAAAAM-MMM!!!!!!! It's out of nowhere for no apparent reason and with sharp aim, someone comes from left field and nails you. You hit the ground, wondering "Why!? What did I do? Why is this happening?!?"

The restaurant business is the most unpredictable-predictable business in the world. I know it's a bit of a tongue twister, but hear me out. I've been in this industry for over 30 years and still I have to deal with so much that is happening daily that sometimes I wonder why I'm still doing it. You could be the best operator, the most competent chef, and/or like I am—a junky to the thrill of pain and the never-ending addiction to do more and more every day—and still you'll have to deal with many problems and so much that can possibly go wrong.

Sometimes you actually do wish someone really punched you in the face.

When I was 18 and opened my first restaurant, my father asked me, "Fabio, are you sure you want to do this? I heard the restaurant business is a pain in your ass." My father's experience doesn't come from food service or hospitality, but in Italy, my family knew a lot of people in the business. He told me to think twice about it because it is harsh.

I can tell you that after 30 years and opening over 40 restaurants, I can only wish that the pain was only located in my ass.

Nevertheless, hospitality is a beautiful business. And do you know why it is beautiful? Because of people like Ken McGarrie.

Ken and his vast hospitality knowledge are a powerful buffer between me and any problem that is about to hit me. Admittedly, he doesn't know that much about food and still eats too much McDonald's. (He's also forbidden to edit out this part.) He is, though, the exact person who should write a restaurant management book. When it comes to motivating genuine hospitality and developing great managers, Ken is one of the best experts and leaders I have worked with.

Early on, he mastered the most valuable lesson in hospitality, which is to *anticipate* and never to *react*. Whoever lives in reaction will always be late to the party. If you don't see it coming, you'll always get sucker punched.

Ken is like a rearview mirror and a crystal ball. He is a rock-star version of a hospitality Nostradamus. Ken can help forecast the stuff that will hurt and make you professionally cry and fix them before it's too late. Of course, sometimes crazy stuff still happens, because Ken's still human after all, despite his godly knowledge.

In the more than six years I have known him, Ken has been talking about publishing this book. Come to find out, he has been working on it for even longer. That's not to say Ken is a procrastinator. Far from it. The reason that it has taken so long has been his dedication to partnering with others, including me, to build great restaurants. For starters, we opened 12 restaurants together in 15 months. That's insanity, but we still did it.

People have a natural tendency to trust Ken because he is incredibly sincere and has a passion for the industry. He is on the ground weeks before an opening, educating the front of house (FOH) staff and instructing managers. I always rest easier knowing Ken is around but not too easy. I mean, it still is a restaurant opening after all.

Of course, we have bumped heads on a few things. That just comes with the territory. The chapter he wrote on "Boulder Theory" (Chapter 23) was inspired by multiple conversations that we have had over the years. He is definitely more prone to caution, whereas I enjoy being very bold. That contrast is one of the reasons we have been so successful together. It's a good balance. Ken is right 90 percent of the time, and the other 10 percent is always a spectacular argument.

When I win an argument, he pouts. But when he wins, he spares me the "I told you so." That's a good dude there.

The other thing about Ken is that he writes really long emails. I mean, "Shoot me already" long emails—some of them are legit novels themselves. So I am very familiar with his writing. Just like he is in person, Ken's style is smart, funny, and approachable. He's also a jerk in a good way. He can tell you to *"BLEEP OFF!"* and you will truly be looking forward to the trip.

Along with his vast expertise, it's his tone and approach that makes *The Surprise Restaurant Manager* such a practical guide. Your restaurant, staff, and guests will be glad you picked up this book.

I love you, Ken! Thanks for all the years of friendship, hard work, and dedication, even when you knew there wasn't a dime to be made. This book will kick asses—or at least prevent a few from getting theirs kicked by this business.

God Speed.

Fabio Viviani

HOW DID THIS HAPPEN?

How do people suddenly find themselves running a restaurant? One minute you're a carefree bartender, successful server, or maybe a comfortable retiree; the next, you are in the middle of the dining floor during a rush juggling the expectation of both staff and guests. Whereas it is a lifelong dream for some, many more are thrust into the role of manager by varied circumstances. It happens more than you think.

Unfortunately, such changes are rarely accompanied with sufficient management training. You don't have four years to get a hospitality degree, and even having that background does not really prepare you for what is to come. You are already in the trenches.

That's what this book is about. You need answers now because, *Surprise!* You're running a restaurant.

This book will help you to address the common challenges that new, and even established, managers face daily as well as provide strategies to overcome them, including sourcing the right staff, improving your online rating, extracting useful data from guests, and avoiding career-limiting HR issues. You will also learn to manage hostility from others, use strong personality types to your advantage, and appreciate blunt criticism.

I love this industry and find joy in working alongside those who make it their home. The majority are creative and welcoming. Restaurants attract big personalities—including management, chefs, wait staff, bartenders, and the guests themselves—which altogether often makes for great hospitality. We provide employment for people from all backgrounds and from every cross section of society. Few other industries blend high schoolers embarking on their first job with retirees choosing to make it their last.

Most importantly, every new venue provides another opportunity where lifelong relationships can be formed. I met my wife and nearly all of my friends while working with them in a restaurant.

My management experience spans every type of concept: Quick-service outlets, high-energy nightclubs, sport-associated venues, upscale casual restaurants, and award-winning fine dining. Because I love giving guests an unforgettable experience that they'll carry with them long after they leave the restaurant, I cofounded Korgen Hospitality. We specialize in helping owners everywhere reach their maximum potential—both in profit and via the guest experience.

Working with world-renowned celebrity chef Fabio Viviani, we opened over a dozen new concepts nationwide and partnered with some exceptional restaurant groups. I have performed extensive hospitality training with thousands of servers, bartenders, hosts, and at least a hundred managers throughout my career, all of whom seem to have one thing in common: they all chuckle when I talk about my first restaurant job.

I got started in the industry working as a dishwasher and theme restaurant mascot at a well-known kid's pizza chain. The mouse outfit I had to wear was continually damp and sweaty from the last person who wore it. It smelled exactly like you think it does. Though sometimes we were asked to stand outside in the blazing sun to wave at cars, the main requirement was to show up occasionally in the dining room.

As you can well imagine, children would either want a hug or run screaming. Middle-school-age kids were the worst and would smack me like a piñata. I quickly realized that being a dishwasher was an easy target for this odious task of pulling double duty as a mascot. However, I also noticed that the manager never seemed to nominate the cooks to do this. So I began learning the stations and lobbied for a position on the line. Soon, I was making pizzas instead of making appearances at birthday parties in an over-stuffed, smelly costume.

I didn't stay back of house (BOH) for long, and by my next hospitality job, I was working as a server. Then I added bartender to my arsenal. That's when it happened. One minute, I was working at a college-town restaurant, the next I was handed keys and a manager title. I'm not even sure if I wanted it. Instead of standing behind the bar, drinking an occasional Bloody Mary for breakfast...*Surprise!*, I now had responsibilities and zero training.

The Surprise Restaurant Manager contains all the things I wish I knew then. Most of what I now know, I developed the hard way by doing it wrong the first time. So please enjoy learning from my countless mistakes.

Before we start, here are two things to keep in mind.

First, I use the names "Todd" and "Amy" as pretend staff members throughout the book. They bear zero resemblance to actual Todds and Amys I have met along the way. So if one of these characters happen to be your name, then you are in for a treat.

Second, and more importantly, I must acknowledge an obvious omission. Although much of the philosophy here is applicable to restaurant management as a whole, the perspective is written from an FOH point of view. It's simply because it is what I know best and have spent my entire career learning. I have tremendous respect for chefs. I also have a fair amount of jealousy because I know I cannot do what they do. If a FOH manager has a solid work ethic, outgoing personality, and empathetic instincts, they can be trained to be great. On the other hand, exceptional chefs are born and are no different than any other creative artist. You can train someone to be a functional cook but it requires inherent talent to craft a remarkable menu. Plus, chefs also get to basically wear pajamas to work, so I envy that too.

CHAPTER 1

WHY ARE YOU RUNNING A RESTAURANT?

You took the manager role because you thought it would provide more opportunities than your hourly position. *Surprise!* Now you are working twice as many hours for half the pay. Sometimes, you wonder why you stopped bartending. What should you do?

Choosing to manage a restaurant is like deciding to go to boot camp: You are committing to a challenging endeavor in order to progress to something greater. Your goal might be to become a GM, transition to other hospitality roles, or possibly open your own restaurant. Focusing on your motivations provides strength when facing struggles and returns joy when accomplishing your goals.

The following scenarios allow you to anticipate the level to which you can expect to be surprised by a manager position. Which scenario best describes you?

TIMED OUT:
Surprise Level: High

You were in an hourly position—likely a bartender, server, or host. The job was meant to be a stopgap while pursuing other career paths. Perhaps, you considered the role of restaurant manager as a fallback if your career in entertainment didn't pan out. And when those aspirations failed to materialize, you turned to restaurant management as an alternative that offered more longevity. You know that you secretly despaired of becoming that club bartender in their forties.

You are also motivated to get to the next level, although more so for financial reasons. In moving from a tipped hourly role, you are not making the same compensation as before.

FAMILY BUSINESS:
Surprise Level: Medium

Restaurants have been in your family for years and always were a part of your life. You are now obligated to run the place. Although you might have hoped your brother or sister was saddled with the responsibility, you knew the family business might come to rest on your shoulders.

You do not have formal training, but you know the restaurant itself better than most of the staff. Now, your objective is to see whether you enjoy the industry.

VANITY PROJECT:
Surprise Level: High

You were very successful in other professions and likely near or have achieved retirement. You always thought it would be fun to have a restaurant so you opened one as a hobby.

What you considered a fun diversion is now eating away at your bank account. You have determined that you need to spend more time in the venue to figure out how to improve operations. You are working in an industry in which you have little experience.

Your goal is to make enough profit so you can hire someone else to run it so you can get back to the golf course.

EMERGENCY FILL-IN:
<u>Surprise Level:</u> High

You were working in other departments (chef, events, marketing, HR) but have been asked to help bridge current gaps in operations. Although you acknowledge the need for assistance, managing a restaurant has never been a dream of yours.

You are hoping this stint is temporary, but you still want to be effective before returning to your primary position.

CAREER CLIMBER:
<u>Surprise Level:</u> Low

You made a decision early in life to get into the restaurant business and studied hospitality management in college. Your objective is to either rise up through the rank to multiunit operations or to someday develop a place of your own.

Restaurant management is a necessary step to achieving your dream. As a kid, you were playing "restaurant" while others played "doctor." Formal training provided you a foundation for understanding operations.

Now you are looking to improve your skills in order to move to a more senior role.

THE CULINARY ROMANTIC:
<u>Surprise Level:</u> Medium

You love to cook and have always dreamed of opening your own restaurant. The thought of providing your community with amazing food and service is exciting, and you have spent years planning what you would love to have on the menu. You want to create the newest hot spot in town and enjoy the fame that accompanies it.

You are passionate about the culinary aspect but far less so about the operational requirements of the restaurant. You enjoy working in the kitchen but find yourself struggling to embrace FOH operations.

WHY YOUR REASON MATTERS

Keeping your motivations in mind will help to alleviate some of the more demanding aspects of management. Running a restaurant is deceptively challenging. You are required to stop by tables where people are eating and ask them how they are enjoying their meal. You are obligated to remain calm when dealing with irrational guests claiming their nonexistent reservation was deleted by a vindictive host. You work long hours on the floor followed by even more time in the office coding invoices, verifying payroll, answering online reviews, and making schedules. You work to inspire your team, most of whom view their employment as temporary until they get "a real job."

But this is *your* real job. And now that you understand "why" you find yourself running a restaurant, you can use this knowledge to help shape the "how."

Surprise! Chapter Review:
Six Categories of Restaurant Managers

1. Timed Out: You are worried about being the oldest bartender in the nightclub.

2. Family Business: Your parents did it, so now you have to as well.

3. Vanity Project: It seemed like an easy retirement idea.

4. Emergency Fill-In: This isn't your job. You are just keeping the seat warm.

5. Career Climber: You went through school but didn't learn all the ropes.

6. The Culinary Romantic: You are in love with creating a delicious menu and becoming famous.

Bottom Line: Understanding why you are running a restaurant will keep you focused on your end goals and provide motivation when you face common challenges.

CHAPTER 2

DON'T HIRE THESE PEOPLE

You never thought it would be this hard to find quality staff. So many applicants seem promising during the interview but once hired, they simply under deliver. *Surprise!* You are constantly dealing with team members arriving late, showing little self-awareness, or being generally negative. What should you do?

Think about how many hours a week you are around "work" people. It's way more time than you are spending with good friends or even those few family members you actually like. So it's smart to be very particular when selecting your team, not only for the functionality of your business but also for your general sanity. If interviewees are knowledgeable, engaging, and confident, they likely will move to the next phase. Are they a good choice?

If only there were red flags to signal the probability of negative tendencies and poor performance in advance. Fortunately, there are, and those warnings actually emerge within minutes of your initial meeting. If you witness any of the following eight offenses, you might want to strongly consider whether to bring them aboard. I have listed them in descending order of severity, from questionable mistakes to outright offer-killers. Be on the lookout for them.

#8: No Resume or Pen: Showing up without either a resume or a pen shows a lack of preparation. Just because they emailed their resume to you does not mean you have taken the time to print it, nor should they expect you to do so. Part of hospitality is anticipating others' needs.

If you are required to read their resume on your phone or computer throughout the meeting because they weren't organized enough to bring a hard copy, it inevitably reduces eye contact, which reveals much unspoken information about an applicant. Such distraction is particularly problematic because other important concerns might pop up in your in-box during the interview, further averting your focus and possibly leading to a hiring mistake. Applicants truly interested in the position will anticipate the need to bring a pen in order to complete some employment paperwork, and your having to source a pen for an applicant is not great.

#7: Improper Attire: Dressing for the job starts with the interview. Obvious candidate errors include workout gear, sneakers, and ball caps. Depending on the restaurant, a suit and tie can be nearly as off-putting. Casual concepts appreciate trendy, contemporary fashion, while overdressing is a sign they didn't do proper research.

The candidate should know enough about the position to foresee the attire worn. Not doing so should raise concerns whether the applicant will fit your culture.

#6: Bringing an Audience: Having a friend drive to the appointment might make an interviewee feel supported, but asking the friend to wait in the restaurant is codependence. It should make you envision their buddy hanging out in your restaurant every day, distracting the applicant from their responsibilities, because it is a distinct possibility. I mean, they brought an audience to the interview. Who does that?

#5: Lying About Termination: There is an unfortunate stigma surrounding being fired. Sometimes, a previous job just wasn't a good fit. Unfortunately, many people clumsily attempt to cover it up in an interview.

It would be refreshing for an employer to hear the truth and a simple reason why. Restaurants offer employment to a broad spectrum of people, including those who might be attempting to overcome previous mistakes. Be open to those who are forthright about a challenging past and avoid those who attempt a cover-up. If someone is willing to be straightforward about being terminated, you should be impressed with their honesty.

#4: No Homework Beforehand: Walking into an interview, a candidate should already know several points about your restaurant, all of which should take no more than 30 minutes to review. Merely glancing at your website is woefully insufficient and, worse, demonstrates mediocrity.

At the very least, they should have:

- Viewed all available menus.

- Read several guest reviews online.

- Examined social media posts (Instagram, Facebook, LinkedIn, etc.).

Use those areas in your questions to candidates.

Most importantly, they should have visited your place and more than once if they're truly interested. How would anyone truly know if they were a right fit without taking the time to check it out first? It's like buying a car without a test drive. Both seem foolish and a bit desperate.

When you find a candidate who did visit, ask them to speak to the positives and touch on a few opportunities for improvement. A few examples show they were paying attention. However, too much negativity will signal that the applicant is quite judgmental and probably not a good fit.

If your place is a new concept and research material on your restaurant is sparse, above-average candidates will have checked out a few direct competitors elsewhere. If you are opening a brand new BBQ place, a great candidate will do some research to see if other BBQ joints are in the area. This effort shows a solid level of commitment and interest on the part of the candidate.

#3: Being Late: Plain and simple, an applicant showing up late for an interview means they will do the same for work. It is disrespectful, unprofessional, and completely avoidable.

The same old "traffic" excuse is almost always offered, as if it is somehow an acceptable reason. It absolutely is not. They should have left their house one full hour earlier than needed, taking the extra time to prepare for the interview nearby.

Showing up too early is nearly as bad as being late. It still shows a lack of respect for your time and an inability for them to schedule themselves accordingly.

#2: Bashing Previous Restaurants: The applicant obviously has reason to be searching for a job, and it's probably due to their previous place of employment.

"Why are you leaving (or have left) your current job?" is a basic interview question you should ask.

If it is a truly unfavorable place to work, a candidate might be tempted to justify their departure by disparaging their previous restaurant. Such statements say far more about the candidate than about their previous employer. It shows the individual is willing to step on the reputation of others to make themselves look better.

I often encounter interviewees who provide borderline slanderous allegations about their previous employers during our conversations, such as drug consumption, rat infestations, sexual assaults, and money laundering. Such occurrences definitely are reasons to seek other employment, but listing those faults just makes the applicant look like a gossip.

Instead, look for an applicant who focuses on the positives and new opportunities that may be available at your restaurant, such as different cuisines, elevated service, and a reputable training program.

#1: No Two-Week Notice: Anyone who is willing to provide less than two weeks' notice to their current employer is unworthy of hiring. If a person will cheat on someone else to be with you, they will cheat on you to be with the next person. See it for what it is: a 100-percent offer killer.

REFERENCES

A quick note about references. Do not make the mistake of only calling the names and numbers provided or merely trusting the recommendation offered by the candidate in writing. Applicants obviously will not lead you to negative information, so you will need to do some digging. Call their previous locations and speak with managers who might not be on their list. Although many companies have a policy of not divulging much information during a reference call, you can usually tell in the manager's tone if the applicant was a quality team member.

Also, if the references they provide list coworkers or others who were not their direct supervisor, see it as a definite red flag.

Finally, avoid hiring someone out of desperation. It is like going to the grocery store hungry: You are going to make bad decisions and buy three boxes of Funfetti brownies. Perhaps, more importantly, always be open to meeting with applicants, even if you are fully staffed. This practice keeps the current team alert and helps to minimize last-minute hires. By not staffing in a rush, you will be able to better spot the eight warning signs of a bad candidate.

Surprise! Chapter Review:
Eight Offer Killers When Interviewing Applicants

1. No Two-Week Notice = Doesn't care about how their actions affect others.

2. Bashing Previous Restaurants = Embraces only negativity and gossip.

3. Being Late = Cannot show up on time for the first day; won't most other days as well.

4. No Homework = Cannot be bothered to walk into the restaurant beforehand or know anything whatsoever

about the place.

5. Lying About Termination = Unwilling to accept reality; would rather rationalize.

6. Bringing an Audience = Their personal life will definitely interfere with their work life.

7. Improper Attire = Has little self-awareness of how they come across.

8. No Resume/Pen = Doesn't anticipate the possible needs of others.

Bottom Line: Applicants absolutely let you know how they will perform on the job during their interview. Learn how to recognize these signs to minimize hiring errors.

CHAPTER 3

QUESTIONS YOU CANNOT ASK

You want to know more about an applicant and wish to connect on similar interests and experiences. You are married and see that the candidate is also wearing a wedding ring, so you consider asking questions about how they met their spouse. *Surprise!* Asking this, and various other questions, would actually be illegal. What should you do?

The best interviews are conversations, a breezy back-and-forth to determine whether working together is a good fit for you both. The first step to leading a quality interview is to avoid the common pitfalls made by so many managers.

ILLEGAL QUESTIONS

There are simply some questions you cannot ask. In fact, these are topics you are unable to discuss by law. Many of them you already know (race, color, religion, etc.), but there are likely a few that might surprise you.

You obviously would not inquire about an applicant's religion or sexual identity, but the questions "Are you married?" or "Do you have kids?" are frequently asked. These are also completely illegal. Your intention might be as innocent as connecting on mutual parenting experiences. Unfortunately, some unscrupulous employers have been known to deny employment to candidates based on their having a spouse or children. The decision is likely due to erroneously assuming the applicant will not have enough time to dedicate to the position.

Other examples of topics and questions to avoid include:

Even if you were in the military and the applicant has a visible USMC tattoo, you cannot ask about their service unless it is listed on their resume, not even if doing so to make a mutual connection or offer appreciation.

You also cannot inquire about someone's age or even make general statements like "We are around the same age" or "We are both from the same generation." Such remarks include referencing birth-related classifications like baby boomer, Generation X, millennial, Gen Z, and so on.

Many states also have outlawed the ability to ask what an applicant earned at their previous job. This intent is to prevent a future employer from paying a candidate less, based on their prior earnings. Paying people based on what they have made in the past has been shown to perpetuate the gender wage gap. Obviously, you should have already budgeted for the position you are attempting to fill and should stick to the number you have already determined.

Topics you cannot discuss and take into consideration when making employment decisions are outlined by the Equal Employment Opportunity Commission, with each state having the ability to add protected characteristics to the list. For example, as of 2021 in my home state of Illinois, these include:

Race, Color, National Origin, Religion, Sex (including pregnancy), Disability, Age, Family Status, Arrest Record, Expunged and Concealed Convictions, Housing Status, Sexual Orientation, Citizenship Status, Ancestry, Military Status, Unfavorable Military Discharge, Protective Order, Military Service or Veteran Status, Protected Medical Condition, Genetic Characteristics or Information, Registered Domestic Partner Status, Sexual Orientation/Trans-

gender Status/Gender Identity.

To find the most current guidelines for your state, visit www. eeoc.gov and your state's department of labor site.

As the interviewer, having this knowledge is definitely an area where you must do your homework in order to avoid an uncomfortable and potentially illegal situation.

CLICHÉ QUESTIONS

Some questions pop up again and again in interviews that are largely worthless and won't really help you to find the best person for the job. They'll only result in giving you the same expected and predictable answers that may or may not even reflect what the applicant truly feels.

Some of the main cliché questions to avoid asking during an interview include:

"Where do you see yourself in five years?"

This inquiry always prompts the answer, "I want to be in a company with growth." Candidates are always wanting "growth," and employers will always claim that they can provide the opportunity.

The problem is who is going to say the opposite? Imagine the applicant who says, "I want a job with no career advancement." Or how about a company that acknowledges, "This is a dead-end position."

"How do you deal with criticism?"

Applicants usually answer promptly with an assertion that they are totally receptive to criticism, while providing zero proof to back up their statement.

However, if you still feel compelled to ask this question, patiently listen to the canned response that you should totally expect to hear, and then ask the applicant for a few specific examples of when they embraced criticism that they received in a previous job and what actions they took to deal with the situation.

"What is your worst quality?"

If you ask this, then you should stand by for any number of silly responses that aren't even really deficits: "I care too much" or "I work too hard."

For once, I would love to have someone answer, "I steal office supplies." I might hire *that* person on the spot for their sheer honesty.

In some cases, many interviewers make the mistake of relying solely on prewritten questions. As an applicant, I was once asked, "Why are manhole covers round?"

It is a fairly typical interview question. The appeal is that there are numerous answers. Square covers could fall through diagonally or leave gaps, but round won't. Round covers are easier to move by rolling. It is easier to dig a round hole than a square one. Whatever the answer, it is supposed to show how a candidate approaches a problem.

Orient questions toward your business. You are hiring based on personality, so try to get applicants to speak about their industry obsessions. For example, ask a bartender what their favorite drink is to make and then have them explain why. Maybe it is the most visually appealing, or offers the highest profitability, or is the easiest to construct. The goal is to find their points of passion and weave the conversation accordingly.

I often ask, "Who does it best? From service to menu to décor, which restaurant stands out to you?" This interchange is an opportunity to discuss positive aspects of another company's values, which lends itself nicely to comparing and discussing those same positive traits in your restaurant.

Being in or at least familiar with the industry, an applicant should have somewhat of an appreciation of other restaurants. How they answer the "who does it best" question will speak to how they view your place. If you are running an upscale steakhouse and the applicant's answer is "Cousin Amy's Chicken and Lobster Shack," then they might not be the best candidate for fine dining. However, if their answer to "who does it best" is *your* restaurant, then you discover that they are a total sycophant.

By the way, the answer I gave as to "why are manhole covers round" question was "because if they were square you would have to call them mansquares." I still got the job.

Surprise! Chapter Review: Five Rules for a Legal and Engaging Interview

1. Never ask a question that might touch on topics covered under EEOC. Check the EEOC list periodically for federal updates (www.eeoc.gov), as well as your state's individual guidelines.

2. Never assume off-limits subjects are safe to discuss if they are brought up by the applicant. Change topics.

3. Always challenge the candidate with thought-provoking questions. If you have heard an interview question multiple times yourself, then you should avoid asking others.

4. Never read straight from a prepared list of questions. They should only be used if you find yourself grasping for conversation.

5. Always focus on personality. If you are enjoying your interaction with someone, chances are your guests will too.

Bottom Line: If you are not sure about whether a question is legal, follow your instinct and avoid. If you are not picking up on a candidate's personality, work to make the interview more thought-provoking.

CHAPTER 4

WHY HOBBIES ARE USEFUL

You have covered the details of an applicant's work history and his/her interest in your restaurant, but you are still at a loss on having a more well-rounded sense of this person and how they might perform in their role. *Surprise!* What should you do?

During interviews, ask about what an applicant enjoys outside of work. This point in an interview is an opportunity to get a better understanding of what motivates them, as well as to extract useful information that might pertain to their desired position.

The following are a few examples, and a completely unscientific opinion, on what a handful of hobbies and activities might say about a job candidate:

- Basketball: understands changing strategies often; works well with a team.
- Tennis: analytical; is self-driven.
- Painting: creative; is willing to be open with expression.
- Bird Watching: observant; has an appreciation of natural surroundings.
- Video Gaming: intensely focused; is goal-oriented.

- Cooking: willing to continually try new things; is unafraid of failure.

- Reading: intellectual; is able to quiet their mind when needed.

- Photography: visual; has an attention to detail.

- Fantasy Football: great with statistics; is a risk-taker.

- Scrapbooking: oriented; is motivated by previous experiences.

- Guitar: patient; is capable of devoting considerable time to achieve even a small level of proficiency.

- Marathon Running: disciplined; has the ability to move well beyond comfort zone to achieve goals.

- Watching Documentaries: pursues educational entertainment; desires to learn more.

You can use those interests to connect the right applicant with their corresponding role. Although there is some crossover, hobbies tend to fall mainly in one of three categories: competitive, creative, and intellectual.

For example:

- Competitive: basketball, tennis, video gaming, fantasy football, marathon running.

- Creative: painting, cooking, photography, scrapbooking, guitar.

- Intellectual: reading, watching documentaries, bird watching.

Competitive roles in a restaurant have a tendency to include servers and bartenders, whereas great chefs often lead with a strong creative drive. The more intellectual positions will likely include human resources and office administrators. This analysis is not an exact science, but it should help you to connect some characteristics with certain positions. Once you have determined their personality type, ask additional questions to verify.

Your only concern should be if an applicant states they do not have hobbies because "they don't have the time." This answer is a clear sign of someone who does not have much balance in their lives, which makes them far more prone to burnout.

Note: if their list of hobbies/interests leads the discussion back to one of the covered characteristics in Chapter 3, make sure to steer the conversation away to safer topics.

VOLUNTEER IMPACT

A job candidate's interests that include volunteer work speaks to their altruism. Those who give of their free time to support others are generally better than the rest of us. Just make sure to take into account their level of commitment. For example, did they do a 5K for an animal shelter once last August, or are they there every week feeding and walking the dogs? Any volunteer work is better than none, but make sure you are rewarding genuine commitment over transparent resume fluff.

Finally, a huge bonus to asking about an applicant's hobbies is that it usually lowers the tension of the interview. They have the chance to discuss the activities they enjoy, and you get to learn about a whole other dimension of their personality. The goal is to bring out more of who they are in a relaxed environment.

You might even be able to connect on a few common interests. You want the applicant to drop their guard and feel comfortable as soon as possible. After that exchange, you want them to be somewhat uncomfortable at other points as well, exhibiting other areas of their personality that will also be helpful for you to experience before deciding whether or not to hire them.

Surprise! Chapter Review:
Four Questions to Determine Type of Hobbies

1. Does it involve keeping score? = Competitive.

2. Is the end result a finished product or skill? = Creative.

3. Is there a learning component to the activity? = Intellectual.

4. Does it primarily benefit other people? = Altruism.

Bottom Line: Explore hobbies to understand what motivates a candidate and make connections on how those interests might translate to their job performance.

CHAPTER 5

CREATING CHALLENGING CONVERSATIONS

You are well into conducting the interview and you like the applicant, yet you are noticing how rehearsed their answers seem. *Surprise!* It's like they got a copy of your questions in advance. What should you do?

Most candidates will arrive already well-versed in the traditional interview format with rehearsed answers to the basic questions about their work history and accomplishments. Therefore, it's your job as the interviewer, and their potential new boss, to change it up a bit.

PUT THE CANDIDATE ON THE SPOT

I am a big fan of role playing. One of my go-to scenarios for applicants is to see how they might coach someone who has improperly set their table. For this, I play the server and ask the applicant to act as the manager.

"It's Monday," I announce, "and during your pre-service walk-through, you notice I have reversed the knife and fork in my section. How do you correct me?" The responses are always illuminating.

Some make a casual correction while helping the server reset properly. They reply, "Do me a favor and please set this section with me. It looks like you inadvertently switched the forks. I will help you so we can do it together faster."

Others go so far as to immediately mention termination. "I see your fork is on the wrong side of the plate!" they exclaim. "Notice everybody else here set their tables correctly. Notice that they also still have jobs. Do you still want to have a job?"

The exercise continues into Tuesday and Wednesday of our fictional workweek here, as I continue role playing the person who just cannot figure out on which side the knife goes. As the issue persists, the applicant must move from corrective coaching to documenting discipline. This scenario is taken all the way to termination, as I have them portray exactly how they would communicate this issue as if it were real.

It is interesting to see how many days of our pretend work-week I, as the server, can go before the applicant, as manager, actually fires me. The record for the shortest is two days. The longest was a week and a half. I didn't hire either of them as neither extreme is acceptable.

You can create similar scenarios for interviewing any position: How a bartender might communicate with fellow staff about overlooked side work, or how a host would address colleagues concerning incorrect reservation procedures. It is useful to learn how someone might communicate with others when problems arise. This game provides insight as to whether the staff will respond well to this person and ultimately uphold the quality and reputation of your restaurant. It's a great exercise to make sure they fit with the culture you have carefully cultivated.

DIVE DEEP INTO THE NUMBERS

Another way to make the conversation more challenging is to investigate arbitrary percentages. For example, if a lead bartender candidate claims to have helped to improve liquor cost of goods sold (COGS) at their previous restaurant by 3 percent, your question should always be "how?"

What was their strategy? Did they mention methods of re-fining portioning, calculation, waste, and theft? Or were they wearing a sandwich board on the side of the highway?

I am not saying these gains are impossible, but they require explanation. It is no different than when a buddy says some-thing inane like, "I'm 90 percent sure..." Where did this magical number come from? It is completely baseless without explana-tion. But you probably don't call out your friends for unfounded percentages. Unless they use the expression "110 percent," and then you shouldn't be friends with them whatsoever.

Challenge candidates on their assertions respectfully. State-ments regarding an increase in sales, enhancement in service, or improvement in costs are always fertile ground to drill down. If they can provide viable answers, then you should probably hire them.

DON'T CORRECT
AN APPLICANT'S MISTAKES

When you encounter these exaggerations during an inter-view, it might be tempting to call the job candidate out on their erroneous information. But you should refrain from addressing flawed responses.

If a guest orders a charcuterie board, calling it "char · cat · tear · ree," you wouldn't correct their pronunciation. At least I hope you wouldn't. It makes you look like an elitist and causes embarrassment to the guest. In fact, you should do the opposite by parroting the mispronunciation back politely when confirm-ing the order.

Same rules apply here. If you uncover flaws in an applicant's assertions or gaps in knowledge, do not call attention to them. When I interview managers, I always ask about optimal cost of goods percentages. When I receive responses like "my liquor cost is 40 percent" or "total labor shouldn't exceed 6 percent," I know they have no idea about realistic COGS. Likely nobody took the time to teach them. If their numbers were closer to standard, I might investigate the source of their figures, but such left-field responses just show up as a miss in their education. As an interviewer, you are not there to teach. Your goal is to learn about the candidate.

I have so much more appreciation for those candidates who simply say "I don't know" than for the ones who make random guesses. They took a stab at the figures instead of admitting a weakness. The applicant already knows they faked their way through your questions. Pointing out their failure will only compound their anxiety and make them feel lectured, on top of not getting the job.

Early in my career, I interviewed for a GM position at an upscale hotel lounge. I was not ready for anything of this magnitude, something I realized almost immediately. I stumbled over every single answer. Five minutes in, the interviewer called another person into the room and they both took turns asking me questions, knowing that I was going to fail.

"Name 10 brands of scotch," one of them said.

I stumbled, mumbling, "Glen…uuuhhh? Glen…eerr?"

The second person interrupted me with a firm "No!" followed by "What about vodka? Can you name at least 10 vodkas?"

It went on like this for another 10 minutes as these guys were shooting smirks at each other. It was their chance to have fun at my expense.

I admit I was in over my head. The interviewer did his job and made our conversation challenging. He rightfully assessed my lack of knowledge and attempts to make up fake scotch names. "Gleningtonson 12 Year" is not a thing.

But once such inexperience became apparent, the interviewer had the opportunity to gracefully acknowledge that it wasn't going to work out. Instead, he brought in an audience for his own amusement and made me feel stupid. **When you are hiring,**

you are in a power position. The ultimate decision always lies with the interviewer. This status comes with the responsibility of being kind and professional.

Make your interviews difficult but respectful. Gather as much information as you can. This occasion might be the only chance you have to dig deep before deciding whether to extend an offer. Just remember that you are sitting across from someone who is considering dedicating part of their career to your restaurant.

Be selective, challenging, and empathetic. Even if not given the job, an applicant will likely make their determination on whether to be a future guest based on your interaction. Needless to say, I never went back to that hotel lounge above where I interviewed. I cannot. It's gone now.

Surprise! Chapter Review: Five Rules for Conducting a Successful Interview

1. Make your interviews difficult. This interaction is not supposed to be an afternoon tea.

2. Question all percentages. Although they look good on paper, numbers on a resume are rarely based in fact.

3. Don't correct factual errors. The applicant is nervous enough without your trying to take them to school.

4. Be empathic and understanding. You have been on that side of the table many times. Remember how that feels.

5. Never forget you have the power. You have the responsibility to make it the best interaction possible.

Bottom Line: An interview is someone's first impression of your restaurant culture. Take the opportunity to make the most of it by providing a supportive, yet formidable, representation.

CHAPTER 6

FINDING GREAT STAFF

You are looking for new servers to join your restaurant. You post a listing on all the traditional job sites. *Surprise!* You are struggling to find quality candidates among responses. What should you do?

Now that you know how to interview, the challenge is finding the "who." It is a proven fact that no restaurant manager in history has ever exclaimed, "Wow, it's really easy to find great staff!" Not once. It is always a constant challenge.

IT'S SO DIFFICULT IN THIS TOWN

I have opened restaurants in a dozen states and one province. In every single venue, managers blamed the location for their difficulty in finding talent. "You don't know how hard it is to find good people in (insert city here)."

Now, when opening restaurants, I often bet my culinary counterparts on when local management will assert this claim, not if. It is a foregone conclusion they will say it. They always do. Do you think it is easier to find better staff in Chicago than New Orleans, Detroit versus Oklahoma City? I can assure you it's not.

I can almost hear your internal monologue right now, wanting to argue that your location is so much harder to find people. You might even point to legitimate challenges like a saturation of competing restaurants in your area, inconvenient transportation options for the staff, uneven volume due to tourism, or unfavorable weather conditions. Although all of those conditions pose obstacles, they are no different than the hindrances experienced by your direct competitors. I am not saying it is easy but you are probably not alone in your struggle.

If you allow yourself to believe the talent pool is light, then you will begin to settle for people who do not meet the standards. Lowering your expectations immediately lowers your service level.

HIRE THE PERSON, NOT THE POSITION

Hire on personality and you are more likely to get the other qualities that are desirable: Genuine positivity, strong work ethic, sense of urgency, pride in one's performance, kindness in all communications. You cannot teach those characteristics. They are inherent qualities. Your only option is to model them yourself and hope others take it upon themselves to emulate.

From a FOH standpoint, a candidate's job experience is truly secondary to their inherent nature. If you are a skilled instructor, you can teach anyone to be exceptional. Servers have to start somewhere. If your training program is solid, they can easily learn with your guidance. When you commit to teaching, you are recognizing that a chosen individual has the capacity to learn something new—and that is a powerful statement that earns loyalty and respect.

Focus on the potential of the candidate more than on the skill set. Be open to all possibilities, then be surprised by whom you discover. A perfect example is a young man who had typically worked as a busser but wanted to bartend at my place. He read every mixology article he could find and spent time getting up to speed. Not only was he exceptional at the position, he was a natural with guests. One year later, when I needed to fill a position in management, he was an obvious choice. Had I only considered his experience, I would have missed out on someone who blossomed into an excellent manager.

CLICKBAIT JOB POSTING

So how do you attract quality people? The most common way to find talent is to post an ad. Whether you are using broad sites like Indeed or Craigslist, or more hospitality-focused options (Hcareers, Culinary Agents), you have to send the right message. The following is an actual post I used for my BBQ restaurant in Canada:

Title: Server Wanted for Bayview BBQ Joint

Subject: (Restaurant name) is a single-location restaurant, started by a couple of people who love BBQ, beer and blues music. We are looking for someone to join our team as a server. Things that set us apart from other restaurants…no bartenders (you make your own drinks), no mandatory tip-out, free staff meals, free uniforms, and you never have to sing "Happy Birthday" to a table…ever. Basically, we treat you like an adult, and in turn, you work as though it were your own place. Eighty percent of the serving staff have been here since Day One so we do not hire often.

If this sounds good to you, email Ken McGarrie at ken.mcgarrie@xxxxx.ca. *Please do not send your resume as they are boring to read. Simply jot down two paragraphs about yourself and interesting things we should know. And no phone calls, please. We look forward to hearing from you.*

Examine the philosophy of the ad. First, the subject line presents exactly what I was looking for, our neighborhood location ("Bayview"), and even conveys the casual nature of the restaurant—calling it a "BBQ Joint." Avoid using vague headers for your ads (example: "A Great Opportunity You Don't Want to Miss This," "Fun Job at a Fun Place") as they are the same come-ons that shady posters utilize.

Next, the ad provides a quick introduction to the restaurant, making it feel independent and exciting. After mentioning the open position again, I launch into several points of difference that make the restaurant an attractive choice. Note that all of them are issues relating to servers. If we were posting for a line cook, I would have highlighted our level of creative freedom, ability to learn smoking techniques, and chance to help build future menu items. Free meals and uniforms are positives for anyone.

The first paragraph ends with a short statement that tells the applicant that this opportunity is a great job and one that doesn't come around often. You never want to oversell in an ad, but you definitely do not want to appear desperate, unless you wish to attract desperate people. Avoid the words "immediate" and "now" in your posts.

The second paragraph is nothing but a test, wrapped in an instruction. The ad commands the applicant NOT to send a resume, NOT to call, and to provide TWO paragraphs about themselves. I chose two paragraphs as there is no set standard to the length of one paragraph. I would not care if it were two sentences separated by a return key; that would be adhering to the guidelines. Out of 100 resumes, if 40 automatically attach a resume, 35 omit the paragraphs, and 15 only write one paragraph, then ignore all 90. They are telling you in advance they won't follow directions. Listen to them.

DAY AT THE FAIR

Job fairs can be a successful way to get in front of a large number of potential hires in a single day. Make sure in your advertisement that you are using the phrase "everyone will get to interview" as oftentimes job fairs just collect applications and don't offer one-on-ones. Have it outside. Bring refreshments and a bag toss. Make it welcoming. And then watch how people react when they are not interviewing.

A sports-related concept has been known to cleverly use job fairs in the past to source candidates. When an applicant arrived, they were told that their interview will take a bit of time to start. Since the venue is built on guests participating in games while eating and drinking, the applicant was invited to join several other "candidates" who are also waiting and currently playing.

The twist is, the others are actually current staff, trained to detect this applicant's personality and report their findings to the hiring manager. If they find someone who joins in, smiles, and makes conversations with others naturally—when they think they aren't being interviewed—they will likely have that same positive energy at the tables. On the flipside, if they just look at their phone, don't talk to others, and don't participate, they will likely bring that distant attitude to work.

BARTENDERS FINDING BARTENDERS

When you are looking for qualified candidates to join the team, the existing staff can be a major help. Ask them to reach out to their friends in the industry. You should offer your team incentives to entice participation. Examples include cash, booze, or the ability to cherry-pick their sections for a week.

I suggest paying out on this reward once the new person has successfully completed training, or perhaps 30 to 60 days beyond. This condition helps to keep the one who made the referral stay connected to the new hire's initial success.

If Todd is your best bartender and he mentions his friend, Amy, whom he swears is amazing, you can definitely benefit from hiring her. I lay a bit of pressure on the existing associate before extending an offer to their buddy. "You know, Todd, you are putting your name on this person, right? " I mention this association to make sure Todd genuinely feels that Amy would be a great addition.

After the new team member has successfully completed training, however, it is important that you thank the original member for their help, after which you must sever all ties of responsibility between the two.

"Hey, Todd, I just wanted to thank you for helping me find Amy. She seems great, and you definitely helped us out on this one. While we are talking about your association with her, I need you to know I understand that Amy is her own person. I'm not going to hold you accountable if she stumbles any more than any other new hire would. I just wanted you to know I appreciate your bringing her in."

You make the comments for several reasons. One, it is obviously not legal to punish a person for someone else's mistakes. Two, you are hedging your bet if Amy turns out to be terrible. The biggest concern about hiring friends of team members is the real possibility that if one is terminated then the other will possibly leave out of protest. That chance is also why you need to separate him from her soon after training, coupled with lots of positive appreciation. If you provide the "judged-as-individuals" talk with Todd too late, then he will likely sense that there is trouble in the water for Amy, even if there isn't, and may harbor guilt for suggesting her in the first place.

Surprise! Chapter Review:
Seven Rules for Finding Quality Staff

1. Never blame your restaurant's location for your inability to find good people.

2. Focus your search on personality over experience.

3. Celebrate your points of difference and culture in your job posts.

4. Test the candidate's ability to follow directions while applying.

5. Do not use job fairs just to collect resumes. Offer guaranteed interviews for all attendees.

6. Use nontraditional opportunities to judge personality.

7. Invite your staff to help source candidates.

Bottom Line: Bring out the personality of your restaurant in your job posting and applicants will show you theirs.

CHAPTER 7

WHY WOULD YOU USE HEADHUNTERS?

You are in need of a chef but are having zero luck with traditional job posts. A hospitality recruiter calls, promising to deliver quality candidates. They offer their services with no guarantee that their chef will be the best fit. *Surprise!* The fee for placing one of their candidates is $7,500. What should you do?

Depending on your role, you might occasionally be in the need for salaried staff, such as managers and chefs. Where is the best place to find them? Posting on traditional job sites is a start.

The problem is that employers who post openings online get a glut of responses from woefully unqualified applicants. There is no gatekeeper preventing the onslaught. Literally, anyone can apply for a manager gig at a bar in Boise, even if they know zero about managing, live nowhere near Idaho, and aren't even old enough to enter a bar. With online posts, there is a lot of hay and very few needles.

On the other hand, restaurants that use recruiters are looking to save considerable time sifting through resumes. That way they are only interviewing candidates who have been carefully vetted.

The headhunting field has expanded tremendously, with some specializing solely in hospitality. They are relatively easy to find. Googling "hospitality recruiters" yields thousands of national firms, and by including a specific city, local options will also emerge.

An important factor in their success is corralling qualified candidates to submit for consideration. Since most recruiters are not paid until they fill a position, it seems like an obvious choice for you to use them. Although I have found tremendous success with recruiters, both as a candidate and an employer, I have also experienced issues that wasted considerable time and money.

Should you use a recruiter?

If your job posts are not yielding the quality candidate you want, you might consider it. If you do not also have a strong network of friends connected to the industry, then you definitely should.

As cliché as it sounds, networking is absolutely vital. Hang out with other restaurant people as much as possible. Embrace any opportunity to make connections. Restaurant association functions are good but so are neighborhood bars where restaurant people hang out after work. The longer you are in this business, the more contacts you will have to source and find top talent or be warned about a potential hire that you should avoid.

RECRUITER CHALLENGES

First, you need to understand a recruiter's business model before you agree to hire them. When a restaurant chooses to work with a placement firm, most contracts stipulate that the recruiters own all resume submissions for up to a year. The recruiter is paid their commission if you hire them within 12 months, even if it is for a different role or a different location within the company. Because of this clause, some headhunters actively blanket their clients with as many resumes as possible as a way to lay claim, regardless of the quality of applicant.

The challenge comes if the same resume is submitted by two

firms. It is your responsibility to immediately alert the second recruiter that you already have that candidate on file. If you exclusively use one firm, tracking duplicate submissions is easier. If you use multiple recruiters to cast a wider net, it can be taxing to manage.

I have seen offer letters pulled off the table because of rival headhunters both demanding payment, all of which could have been avoided if the manager had sorted their in-box better. Fortunately, "spaghetti recruiters" who throw everything at the wall to see what sticks typically fail over time. But they are still out there, so you need to do your homework. Definitely source referrals from other restaurant operators.

It won't take long for you to pinpoint placement firms that simply submit countless resumes for the sake of claiming dominion. They are also likely to skip through pre-interviewing their candidates. Pre-interviews are vital since they establish a job candidate's goals and qualifications. If this step is omitted, the placement firm is more likely focused on commission than on a quality fit for you and your restaurant.

Worthy firms have zero motivation to cram a square peg in a round hole. If the job is a mismatch, it is a waste of everyone's time. You will lose both faith in the recruiter and a substantial amount of money.

THE COST IS HUGE

Commission fees for a placement firm run typically 10 percent to 25 percent of the position's annual salary, depending on the firm. At 20 percent, filling a $60K/year manager position will cost your restaurant an additional $12K. This charge is usually due within 30 days of their start date and with limited guarantees. If a chef quits after a few months or is even fired for cause, you don't get a refund. At best, you might get a credit for a future replacement.

Because of this risk, you should be extra cautious when offering positions to an applicant represented by a recruiter. Most restaurants that use headhunters have at least one horror story about the money they lost by hiring the wrong person.

If you are able to find quality applicants without using a placement service, you will save thousands. It is also important for you to learn to build other sources, particularly internally, where you can find candidates and not just rely on headhunters.

Why would a restaurant use a placement company, given the considerable fees?

Recruiters can contact potential applicants who are currently employed somewhere else. It is a fishing expedition, usually a call or email, saying, "There is a great opportunity available. Do you know anyone who is interested?" The intent is clear. They are seeing if someone might be willing to switch jobs.

If you, as a representative of your restaurant, do that, then it's poaching. This tactic is definitely not appreciated in our industry. On the other hand, recruiters are able to see if a potential candidate is willing to make a change, even without disclosing the name of your venue. They have a reach far beyond a basic job post.

Final verdict: Do both. Retain a recruiter and continue looking on your own. If you do hire through a headhunter, make sure the candidate and the agency are worth the extra money.

At the end of the day, recruiters are sales people. When they place a candidate, they have made their sale. Even though they tell you a candidate is a 100-percent perfect fit, make sure to judge their claim for yourself without being swayed by their comments. Also make sure to draft the final offer yourself to ensure that the recruiter did not misrepresent any of the terms of employment. It ruins trust when there are misunderstandings from the beginning.

Above all else, don't spend all this time and effort locating and hiring someone only to have a culture that prompts them to exit quickly.

Surprise! Chapter Review:
Six Prerequisites for Using Hospitality Recruiters

1. Only use if the quality of applicant on your traditional searches are subpar and you do not have a network of contacts to use for this search.

2. Only use if the recruiter offers a free replacement hire, preferably for up to six months, if the first does not work out.

3. Only use if they have an extensive pre-interview screening for candidates and are sending you notes on their discussions.

4. Only use if you are looking to also target potential applicants who are currently employed.

5. Only use if they have solid industry references and a track record of not sending junk.

6. Only use if you feel they are a true partner to your restaurant and can source candidates you cannot find on your own.

Bottom Line: If you are looking to fill a salary position, reputable hospitality recruiters can save you considerable time and effort. Just make sure you are unable to find the same talent on your own.

CHAPTER 8

ROBOTIC STAFF ALWAYS SHORT-CIRCUITS

You are confident you've hired great servers to join the team for the summer patio season. You have them shadow your top staff for several days. After providing them a table script and the items to push for the day, you release them onto the floor. *Surprise!* They are unenthusiastic and robotic. All the personality you saw in their interviews is gone. What should you do?

We all have encountered robot servers. You know the type. They arrive at your table expressionless. No smiles. They rattle off the ingredients of a few menu items with zero excitement. If you listen closely, you can overhear them giving the exact same speech to the table next to you. And the one after that. It is definitely not captivating service.

In order to achieve superior hospitality, you must instill an appreciation of your restaurant with your staff, the foundation that is established from day one. You hired them largely because you enjoyed their personality and you want your guests to have the same reaction. Your job is to build a genuine love for the restaurant with your team so that they can showcase that affection to your guests. It all starts with being able to enjoy the menu themselves first.

REQUIRE TASTING OF EVERYTHING

I am always surprised at the servers I encounter who have never tried everything on their own menu. You must have your team taste everything. How can you speak enthusiastically about something you have never experienced? You have to expose your staff to everything you have to offer in order for them to fully appreciate your restaurant.

If you are concerned about the financial impact of having your staff try everything, you can touch on a few items during their initial training and then incorporate tastings as part of daily pre-shifts. You should schedule which dishes will be presented and discussed, making sure to cycle through the entire menu each month. This rotation will provide additional exposure for the new crew and serve as a good reminder for the veteran staff.

PROMOTE GENUINE SUGGESTIONS

Most restaurants require their staff to provide suggestions. The reason that you want your team to taste everything is so they can talk about their favorites with authenticity. Everyone should have that one dish on the menu they love more than the others, which should be the item they discuss with their guests.

My favorite menu suggestion ever was at a BBQ restaurant in Rochester, New York. I was alone, sitting at the bar during a crowded lunch rush. The bartender approached, handed me the menu and announced, "Try the beer and cheddar soup, it is like BLEEP-ing crack!"

I love the suggestion because it was honest. The way I saw it unfold, she was setting up her bar and walked past the kitchen, where a cook suggested she taste the soup. At this point, she decided it was the absolute best thing they had to offer and felt duty-bound to let everyone she encountered know about it.

Her suggestion was real and made me want to order it. When she did her two-bite check, she asked what I thought, not because she was required to, but because she absolutely wanted to know if I agreed with her. This check-back is the basis of true hospitality: making genuine suggestions and inquiring because you care.

DON'T PUSH

Your job is not to tell your team what to fall in love with, rather allow them to discover what they love for themselves and encourage them to speak about those dishes with passion. In the case of the New York BBQ joint, there is no way a manager during pre-shift instructed staff to call the soup "BLEEP-ing crack." It was an organic and real response from the bartender herself.

If you require your servers to push items they don't like, it will likely be detected in their service. The obvious sign is the lack of exciting adjectives. When a server is ordered to sell dishes they don't enjoy, they will likely stick to listing the ingredients.

Watch for this distinction the next time you are dining out. Notice if your server's eyes look up when they are recalling a dish. See if they smile, and listen for adjectives. Is the delivery a recipe-based description with locked eyes and an expressionless face? If so, you are being served by a robot.

FOCUS ON ADJECTIVES

The best guest suggestions resemble a conversation among friends. Let's say you take a buddy to a local restaurant where you are obsessed with the brisket mac & cheese. Naturally, you would suggest ordering and likely describing it with positive adjectives. "You have to try it. The brisket is incredibly tender, and it is awesome with mounds of cheese and delicious pasta."

You'd never say to a friend, "I suggest the brisket mac & cheese. Gruyère and Gouda are combined with their housemade elbow macaroni, topped with four ounces of brisket."

Given the option, I would always rather hear the first example from a server over the second. People can always read ingredients on the menu. The server's role is to paint pictures in their guests' minds of how great the dish will be.

Utilize initial training and pre-shift tastings to poll the staff on which adjectives would best describe each item. When asked to sell it back to you, steer them away from simply listing what is in a dish. Remind them to focus on their emotional response.

CONTINUE THEIR EDUCATION

Consider those who complete training as if they were finishing freshman year of college. They made it through the first level but there is much more work needed in order to attain a degree. You must be dedicated to ensuring education does not stop once their beginning training is over.

Beverage reps are a convenient and useful way to keep your staff engaged. Focus on a certain region of wine each week. Host in-depth training on manufacturing and production of different spirits. You can also do the same with food vendors, particularly if they practice humane harvesting of livestock, support sustainable or organic farming, or are locally sourcing ingredients. The more information you provide, the more your staff will appreciate your dedication to continuing to learn.

You could conduct voluntary management classes. Maybe some of your staff are considering a career in the restaurant industry. You can give them a leg-up by teaching aspects that they probably don't know. The subjects could include learning to read a profit and loss (P&L) statement, building labor forecasts, leveraging multiple vendors for best pricing, or anything you feel you can share. Such extras show that you are personally invested in their continued success.

Finally, field trips are a good idea, combining instruction with staff bonding. The plan can be anything from touring a local brewery to travelling to a different part of the world. Just make sure to invite everyone, as it will rightly foster resentment in those who were left out.

Although the educational portion is important, these excursions reinforce the ultimate goal: Having a team who truly cares about the restaurant. It is hard to be unenthusiastic about your job if you just returned from an enjoyable road trip.

Overall, the key to ridding your restaurant of robots is to focus on making your staff truly excited to be there. By asking them to have a passionate voice in their suggestions and investing in their ongoing education, your team is more likely to love their job, which will be ultimately evident to your guests. Robots are incapable of love.

Surprise! Chapter Review: Five Ways to Avoid Robots

1. Have continual tastings for staff.

2. Encourage recommendations based on honesty.

3. Never require staff to only push certain dishes.

4. Value passionate adjectives over straightforward ingredients.

5. Offer educational opportunities weekly or at least regularly.

Bottom Line: Focus your attention on the staff's buy-in and appreciation for the restaurant, and it will definitely improve service.

CHAPTER 9

HOW TO LOSE GOOD PEOPLE

Every week it seems like someone else quits at your restaurant. When you ask why they are leaving, most only tell you that they found work elsewhere. The exodus is way too much to be a coincidence. *Surprise!* Now you are spending all your time trying to hire new people. What should you do?

Your staff will quit for a multitude of reasons. Maybe your place is bar-focused, and they prefer a more chef-driven concept. Perhaps, they underestimated the scope of what the position required. Most often though, it is not the venue that makes people leave but those in charge of running it.

When you become a manager, you set the tone. Everything you say and do is watched and evaluated. You are not just one of the team anymore.

A well-known restaurant boasts exquisite dishes and flawless service. It is a magnet for celebrities and packed every night. The staff earns great money. So why does it have such a high turnover? The answer can be found in the way management communicates. Those staff who endure operational negativity or lack of good communication do so merely for the paycheck, which tends to be less motivating as time wears on.

The question then becomes: Do the restaurant managers recognize how their behavior is affecting their team? More importantly, are *you* making similar mistakes?

The following five questions will help assess if you are associated with, or are even contributing to, a bad restaurant environment.

Do you believe everyone around you is perpetually terrible? Sounds like: "I think Todd doesn't care. He sucks."

Such comments often are opinions, which can be changed with the right approach. Your tendency to be critical might come from a belief that you keep others on their toes. Quite the opposite; it motivates them to avoid you whenever possible.

Your comments will also build resentment among those who feel they are working their hardest. If your staff is always receiving a barrage of negativity, they will also naturally translate that same energy onto the floor. Motivation drives results. Constant negativity will ensure that your staff, and ultimately the restaurant, does not meet full potential.

You should always "praise in public; correct in private." This practice will provide more effective coaching, instead of aiming to shame others into performing better. Also, you should always lead from facts: "I have noticed that Todd's check average and tip percentage have both declined in recent weeks."

Are you habitually threatening terminations? Sounds like: "If you don't improve, you are not going to have a job here."

"Churn-and-Burn" shops, which are restaurants with high turnovers, foster a culture of fear. This ill-advised tactic sometimes works in the beginning to make the staff feel high standards are being established. As your warnings become more commonplace, they learn to dismiss them as the idle rants of a loose cannon.

Certainly, logical reasons exist for removing people who are detrimental to the team, but such decisions should occur after multiple coaching sessions and clear directions for improvement. When that staff member was hired, you saw potential for greatness. Were you wrong then or are you wrong now?

Do you remind the staff how "lucky" they are? Sounds

like: "I have a stack of applications from people who would love to have your job."

Do you use team meetings to announce how poorly they are doing and how fortunate they are to work there? This tactic is usually coupled with the obnoxious claim that you have applicants waiting in the wing. The truth could not be further off. You know how many interviews you conducted just to find your current team. Remember, when your team wakes up each day, they each make a choice to stay or take a job somewhere else. Great people can find work anywhere. Their willingness to remain with you is something you should recognize with appreciation regularly.

Regardless of someone's performance, it is important to treat them with respect and not only for the staff member you are trying to coach or show the exit door. Remember that everyone is watching you and that showing respect to all affects the culture overall.

Are you visibly upset during service? Looks like: clenched teeth, big hand gestures, and obvious frustration.

There is no reason to address the staff negatively on the floor. Let's say you witness long ticket times, a bottleneck at the host stand, and tables needing to be bussed. How often do you meet such situations with a look of distress and anger in the middle of the dining room?

If there is a failure in the midst of service, your best approach is to help. You can address issues later in a subsequent pre-shift or staff meeting. Yelling in the moment accomplishes nothing and is truly demoralizing to your team in front of guests.

Do you act like the guest is always right? Sounds like: "That guy is a regular. Don't worry about what he said to you."

As much as it is important to appreciate your guests and work to accommodate their requests, sometimes their behavior will clash with your team. These instances include rude or abusive comments or even physical actions directed toward staff. When met with conflicts, do you usually take the side of the guest? You shouldn't.

Some guests treat FOH staff like servants, calling them inappropriate names or placing their hands on them. Usually, such people never had a job in the restaurant industry or they'd know better. A guest can absolutely create a hostile work environment, and if you do not address their poor behavior, you are complicit in fostering it. You also will drive your staff away in droves.

Try to remember what it was like to be in your staff's positions. Keep it light, yet consistent. Most of all, work to support your team the right way during service.

Surprise! Chapter Review:
Six Ways to Rid Your Restaurant of Great Staff

1. Threaten to replace team members if they fail.

2. Be noticeably upset often, especially on the floor.

3. Tell your staff how fortunate they are to work for you.

4. Admonish staff in public vehemently, making sure everyone sees you hand out punishments.

5. Nitpick, pointing out your frustration with others who are incapable of anticipating precisely what you want.

6. Value your guests more than your staff.

Bottom Line: Creating a welcoming, positive environment for your team is the best strategy to eliminate high turnover and improve hospitality. If your staff is not happy to be in your restaurant, your guests will surely notice, especially when team members are no longer working there.

CHAPTER 10

SLEEVES UP OR DOWN

You made countless drinks in your day as a bartender, so you are quite confident you know the best way to help out in a rush is to jump behind the bar. You are a hands-on leader and believe the solution is always stepping in to assist. *Surprise!* The way you are trying to help is actually causing more of a headache for your staff. What should you do?

How do you support your team during service? Are you more likely found in the dish pit washing forks or on the floor pointing out problems for others to fix? Do you "roll your sleeves up" and jump behind the bar at a moment's notice, or are you "sleeves down" with a tendency to assign tasks to others?

Although many gravitate toward one side or the other, effective leadership requires an equal balance of both.

ROLLING UP YOUR SLEEVES

The "sleeves up" manager places paramount value in working alongside staff. You notice dishes accumulating in the busser station and run them to the kitchen. If there is a table that hasn't been reset, you do it yourself.

This tendency is not an inherently negative instinct; it is just not always the most productive.

Your assistance delivers a temporary solution but does not build a permanent one. If plates are piling up and table flips are lagging, it's happening more than you think. If you are always having to "roll up your sleeves," it is due to improper hiring, training, or scheduling, all of which are within your control.

As a manager, your attention must be on long-term systems over short-term responses.

That's not to say you shouldn't help out, just do so where you will have the greatest impact on service, not on the flow of staff. In the same way that you don't go on the line to prepare steaks, you should not be behind the bar attempting to make drinks. If the pantry chef has stepped off the line and you are the only one free to make a Caesar salad, go for it. If the only bartender is in the restroom and you are watching service tickets pile up, step in to assist. Your help is better than nothing.

Filling in for a missing team member is different from "jumping in" when the full staff is present and experiencing an unexpected volume. Let's say, due to several large-party walk-ins, the restaurant is experiencing a major rush. If you are a "sleeves up" manager, you might be tempted to hop in to serve drinks. Unfortunately, you are naturally less efficient than a regular bartender. Instead of having a knowledgeable cross-trained server assist, you plant yourself in a very visual spot as if to say, "Look, I'm helping!" You are likely interrupting as much as you are alleviating.

"Sleeves up" managers definitely believe they are being useful. When questioned by their boss about what happened with the ticket times last night, the likely answer is, "We were slammed. I was helping make drinks for hours!" This response is merely code for "Don't blame me, I tried."

Instead of attempting to bartend, the manager should have been communicating with guests affected by the service issues and working to salvage their experience, while crafting immediate strategies for improvement. That way, the question of why ticket times were long would receive a detailed explanation accompanied by an action plan. The following is an example:

Issues: The wine was not fully stocked, causing delays in service. We also experienced a surge of walk-ins and flat-sat the room at 7:00 p.m., which put the bar underwater at 7:15 and the kitchen at 7:45.

Solutions: The opening bartenders have been alerted to walk the bars daily to check pars, and I have scheduled a host meeting this Friday to address strategies to pace the book when encountering a large amount of walk-ins. Chef and I spoke about better communication with the kitchen during volume and will work to radio open menu counts every 15 minutes, slowing the door as needed.

You cannot provide solutions for the entire restaurant if you have your "sleeves up" solely in one section. Instead of attempting to make cocktails, you should deliver them, taking the opportunity to engage with your guests.

The same logic applies when in the kitchen. FOH managers love to stand in expo and congratulate themselves on how much they are helping. The fact is the best runner can likely out-expo you any day. You should be bringing food to tables and inquiring about the guests' experience. Don't stand behind the host desk; grab menus and seat people.

These tasks have the greatest impact without being obtrusive to your team. This practice also allows you to be mobile, supporting each section for a bit, while observing the restaurant as a whole.

KEEPING YOUR SLEEVES BUTTONED

The flipside is obviously "sleeves down," which is the manager who assigns tasks to others.

This one is harder to master because it does not come as naturally. Delegation is a vital component of management, as it allows you to continue monitoring other aspects of the restaurant. It also helps your staff to learn best habits, and it shows trust in your team. If you are consistently asking the bussers to dim the lights at 8:00 p.m., the goal is that they will begin to do so at some point without prompting. Unfortunately, if delegation is done incorrectly, it is worthless as a communication tool or as a means for accomplishing anything.

How often have you assigned a task only to find it incomplete later? Was it met with frustration with whomever you asked? As in, "Amy, I told you to reset that table 10 minutes ago, and you still haven't done it." The blame for why the table is a mess has less to do with Amy and more with you. From the way you asked, to the all-important follow-up, there is a method you must adopt to be efficient. When you ask your staff to perform a specific task, always wrap it with: "May I ask you a favor?" and a sincere round of "Please" and "Thank you."

Sounds pretty basic, right? It is, yet this simple and powerful act of leadership is often ignored, especially during a rush.

In the above scenario, proper communication is: "May I ask you a favor? Please quickly reset table 12?"

Yes, you are their boss; you could simply tell them to do it. But that approach just doesn't build a very positive environment.

Great people become less motivated when managers demand instead of ask. You both know it isn't really a "favor," but it gives the appearance of choice, which is always appreciated.

Once you have delegated, the key is to follow up on whether the request has been accomplished. If so, you circle back around to the staff member and thank them for completing it. "Hey, Amy, thanks for taking care of that." Now you know the table has been reset, and it has the added benefit of applying an extra layer of appreciation for the server. She registers that you acknowledge the effort and you are able to take it off your mental to-do list. If it hasn't been completed in a timely manner, you reengage with a bit more assertiveness but still with a "Please" and "Thank you."

For example: "Hey, Amy, I still need you to please take care of table 12. Thank you."

Again, given ample time, you must see if the task is complete. If so, you still thank them the same as you would before, as it reinforces positive behavior.

FINDING YOUR MIDDLE

Striking the correct balance between sleeves-up and sleeves-down management takes time. Delegate too much and you appear lazy; not enough and you are ineffectual. If you are looking to find the middle, try the following exercise.

Find a simple task that requires attention from your staff. It might include pre-bussing a table, cleaning the floor, or wiping down the bar. Begin doing it and then wait to see who takes it out of your hands. If you are sweeping the sidewalk and a host approaches and says, "Here, let me do that," then let them do it. You have then successfully delegated without having to assign.

More importantly, you now know which staff members are willing to help and those who just watched you sweep with their arms crossed. If you do this periodically, you will have a better understanding of your team, while supportively communicating standards.

FOUR ESSENTIAL WORDS

Have you ever noticed how few staff members actually request *your* help?

Picture this: It's Friday night. The line is out the door, the service bartender is in the weeds, servers are near-jogging between tables, and bussers are all furiously working to reset.

You ask everyone, "Do you need help?"

And you are met with a chorus of "Nope" and "I've got it."

But yet "yes," they do need your help because they obviously don't "got it!" Even worse, you can see the problem by the dissatisfied, and even angry, looks from the guests.

So why won't they ask for assistance? The answer is in your approach.

Many assume that soliciting help is a weakness, prompting you to think they are incapable and risking a reduction of their section. Their fear is not unfounded, as more than a few ill-equipped managers have the mentality of "just handle your tables." This approach only stifles open communication, prompting the staff to cover up service errors for fear of punishment, leaving the guest to deal with a poor experience without the benefit of management intervention.

Such a scenario is why you must develop a culture where it is praised to raise your hand. Most importantly, you as the manager need to appear accessible.

When you ask, "May I help you?" add these four words: "I have the time."

This approach always works to lower staff's hesitancy to accept assistance. Adding "I have the time" reassures the person that you are completely available to them in the moment. Just be prepared to provide the assistance you have offered, free of judgment. As a staff member, it takes strength to ask for help. As an effective manager, you must be dedicated to always responding with supportive action.

Surprise! Chapter Review:
Six Rules to Make Sure Your Help Is
Actually Beneficial

1. Always focus on the tasks that support the guests when you roll up your sleeves.

2. Never take the opportunity to assist only as a way to show others that you helped.

3. Never get locked into one area. Stay mobile on the floor.

4. Always follow up to check completion on tasks you have delegated.

5. Always use your nice words. Never point or bark.

6. Always add "I have the time" when asking if someone needs help.

Bottom Line: Truly helping your team does not always require rolling up your sleeves. It also does not mean to delegate every task either. Striking the proper balance is a skill you should pursue daily.

CHAPTER 11

WITNESS PROTECTION

You have a server who continues to set their tables incorrectly. You have coached them multiple times on the floor on proper procedures. Instead of being receptive, they have become increasingly defensive. Their behavior now requires a documented warning. You call them to your manager office. *Surprise!* Although you think the conversation was productive, the server tells the owners you were verbally aggressive. What should you do?

Lack of proper communication always tops the list of reasons people seek new opportunities, so it is your responsibility as the manager to continually coach your team. This task should happen daily, providing insights and encouragement in the moment. If you observe a particular area requiring improvement, addressing it can often be easily communicated on the floor.

Unfortunately, there are times you will need to have a more structured conversation with a staff member. You have counseled him or her on several occasions about improvement, and now an elevated communication is required. This discussion might incorporate verbal or written documentation, final warning, or even termination. Whenever you are going to deliver challenging information, which does not fall in the parameters of in-the-moment coaching, you must have a witness in the room.

WHO MAKES A GOOD WITNESS?

A witness could be a fellow manager, executive chef, or owner—anyone who is in a full management position. This choice should never be a fellow staff member because they work alongside each other and are not in a position of authority. The best option would be someone who functions as HR for your company, as they should have specific training in proper staff communication. On the other hand, a person not connected to your restaurant would not be a good choice. You obviously would not want to ask your liquor rep to watch you critique a server.

THE RIGHT TO REMAIN SILENT

Remember that a witness is present equally for both parties. In the event that either side acts inappropriately, the witness is able to report this behavior. You never wish this situation to be perceived as two-on-one, so make sure you select someone whose presence will be appreciated. You never want your staff member to feel like you and the other person are ganging up on them. It is for this reason the witness should remain silent, except if they observe misunderstandings and need to facilitate effective communication. Make sure those whom you might ask to be in such a position are informed of their role and responsibility in being present.

ACKNOWLEDGE THE WITNESS

Have the witness sit equally spaced from both parties. Never have them sit on the same side of the table as yours. Before you start, acknowledge why they are in the room. I typically say, "This person is a witness and will not be taking part in our discussion, but you may ask them questions about our conversation if you wish. They are here solely as a third party for the protection of both you and me."

Once the discussion is over, have the witness write down and submit their observations to you. If you need to have a private conversation with a team member and a suitable witness is not available, then postpone the meeting. Do not deliver criticism by yourself. The act is a huge risk.

A CAUTIONARY TALE

I knew a manager who observed one of the bartenders having a shot with a guest, a practice that was not allowed at this venue. He immediately pulled her from her station and brought her to the office. What happened next is up for debate. He claimed she became belligerent and verbally combative. She stated that he asked for sexual favors in exchange for not firing her. No one is really sure what truly happened, but he lost his job and she left on her own soon after. Had there been an impartial witness in the room, someone who was empowered to create a safe environment for feedback, the outcome would assuredly have been different.

Use a witness every time you are having a private conversation with staff. This rule is for everyone's protection.

Surprise! Chapter Review:
Five Rules for Using a Witness Effectively

1. Never use an hourly staff member. Always utilize someone in management.

2. Always select someone who makes the other person feel more at ease. You should focus on their comfort as you are the one in the position of power.

3. Never have the witness sit on the same side of the table as yours. Have them sit equidistant.

4. Always acknowledge the witness' presence at the beginning and the fact that they will not be speaking in most cases.

5. Always have the witness send a follow-up email documenting their observations.

Bottom Line: You must use a witness whenever you anticipate having a challenging conversation with a staff member. The proper choice provides a safe environment for both you and your team to have constructive, honest discussions about performance issues.

CHAPTER 12

HOW TO AVOID HR

On a recent visit to a neighboring restaurant, you overhear several servers within earshot cursing and complaining about a table. In an attempt to make your experience a learning lesson at your own place, you mention the incident during your pre-shift. You include their comments to make your point. *Surprise!* The next day, you are informed of an HR complaint due to the foul language. What should you do?

Want to know what is behind every uncomfortable communication between staff and management? Overestimated familiarity.

I am not talking about coaching sessions on better table maintenance or improving check averages. I mean interactions that make team members uneasy and may ultimately require the intervention of an HR professional.

WHAT IS OVERESTIMATED FAMILIARITY?

Overestimated familiarity is when you communicate with a person in a more casual manner, which they do not appreciate. Regardless of how much you think you are "friends," you still hold power over someone who reports to you, and that status always changes the relationship. You can't be just friends.

For example: Todd, one of your best servers, bears a passing resemblance to a character in *Superbad*, so you call him "McLovin." He might laugh and pretend he enjoys it, but at best, he tolerates the comment because you are his boss. Nobody wants to be called McLovin, not even Christopher Mintz-Plasse. You have made the mistake of overestimating the casualness between you and a specific staff member with no malice intended.

Such actions are not rooted in control or abuse. They are uncomfortable jokes and casual comments that some managers make, based on a desire to be better liked by their team. It's the attempt to be accepted on a social level, rather than a professional one. It is an overcompensation for insecurity, running the gamut from unintended inappropriate remarks to unintentional bullying and discrimination, all of which rightly open the door to HR involvement.

The defense is always the same: "I didn't mean anything by it. Todd is great. He knows that. If he would have told me, I would have stopped."

Every time you overestimate your familiarity with someone, you do so at your own risk.

Many managers measure success by whether they are liked, which typically means addressing the staff in an overly casual manner, incorrectly thinking it makes them more approachable and effective. In your role, you must understand that the scales are never even.

Your staff does not want to be your friend. They want to be respected by you.

You are in an elevated position by definition, and your team will never feel comfortable communicating on equal terms. If "McLovin" thinks you look like a *Simpsons* character, he's probably not going to call you "Homer" because you are still his boss. At least not to your face.

KNOW YOUR AUDIENCE

Let's take a moment to address staff conversations in most restaurants. Not PG-13 to be sure. Much of the chatter centers around busting each other's chops. As a manager, joining in this communication can be truly risky for you personally, the restaurant, and the culture.

While working at a bar, several staff members started calling me "Pelón," which is Spanish for bald. This depiction is accurate. Soon, everyone began to call me this, including my boss.

Fortunately, I was secure at this point with it, but earlier in life that reaction definitely wasn't the case. Nobody wants to go to prom with a comb-over. My GM took a risk by joining in on the nickname. Had I wanted to take the opportunity to complain about her calling me Pelón, I would have had a strong case.

Know your audience. The casual nature of restaurants is one of the reasons most people are attracted to it. But as a manager, if you are not sure if a staff member will appreciate their nickname, or any less-than-professional communication, it is better that you don't join in. Nicknames can actually be considered discrimination and harassment.

Also, just because someone is okay with your using it at the moment does not mean you are safe down the road. Had my GM disciplined me for something that I felt was unfair, I could have potentially leveraged her use of the nickname against her, claiming hostile work environment.

However, my GM read me correctly, and I didn't take offense to the name. To this day, there are people who only know me as Pelón, and I love that fact.

IF HR COMES CALLING

If you are presented with an issue from your HR rep, appreciate the willingness of the team member who complained to bring it to your attention. As much as your surface-level response might be defensive, the reason most people reach out is not vindictive. It is disappointment. Much like online reviews, they feel let down but are reaching out in an attempt to prompt change.

The fear here should not be someone being summoned to HR, as there is an opportunity to learn from the experience. The real concern is if that person walks away permanently and nothing improves.

WHEN A PLAN FAILS

I have had someone speak to HR about me on the subject of hugs, but it's not what you are probably thinking.

I enjoy greeting others with open arms while always being mindful that this trait might be perceived as invasive by some. I never want anyone to feel uncomfortable or pressured to give me a hug. I have encountered managers who initiate required hugging, thinking it makes them more welcoming, unaware how unwelcome it is.

Fact: mandatory touching is always creepy.

So, I devised a strategy to make sure I was never seen as that kind of person. I thought my plan was a perfect solution: I would never initiate a hug, but if anyone came toward me with their arms outstretched, then I rationalized it was fine to reciprocate. No long duration, just a slight connection of shoulders and a quick pat on the back—the kind of hug where you could fit a basketball between us. I accepted hugs from all genders equally, no different than a handshake. Who could have an issue with such impartiality?

Well, I did receive feedback. Interestingly, the complaint had nothing to do with any physical contact I had made, which turned out to be the actual problem. One staff member saw me hugging others and concluded that since I didn't hug them, that I didn't like them.

I had the usual reaction: "I didn't mean anything by not doing it. That person is great. If they would have hugged me, I would have hugged them back."

Without knowing it, I rejected this person—someone whose work was exceptional and whom I appreciated greatly. I was thankful that the individual spoke to HR and allowed me the dialogue to repair the communication. My "clever hug strategy" didn't work flawlessly, and although I never meant to exclude anyone, **intention never justifies actions.**

HR would advise the safest course is to never hug anyone at work, but admittedly I still do. There are simply some people who always welcome me with an embrace, and I would feel awkward if I offered a fist bump instead. That being said, by doing so, I am still taking a chance every time.

My best advice is to be mindful of the possible unintended consequences of your comments and actions and to know that the responsibility for supportive communication with your team is on your shoulders. If you are not absolutely sure, then err on the side of a high-five.

Surprise! Chapter Review:
Six Rules When Faced with an HR Complaint

1. Always understand how difficult it was for someone to speak up, especially about their boss.

2. Always consider how uncomfortable and nervous the complainant feels.

3. Always appreciate their willingness to attempt to rectify the situation.

4. Always be willing to apologize. No matter your intention, their perception was negative.

5. Never attempt to follow up and further address with the complainant afterward. They are attempting to move on from the matter, same as you.

6. Never discuss the matter with anyone else. Breaking confidentiality will definitely shutter your open-door policy.

Bottom Line: The more you focus on being liked, the more likely you are to engage in overestimated familiarity.

CHAPTER 13

THE ART OF TERMINATION

It is time to fire Todd. There have been too many errors, and your multiple coaching efforts have been unsuccessful. *Surprise!* You don't have much experience with terminating staff and are worried about how to execute correctly. What should you do?

Terminations are not enjoyable, but they are essential—to be used as a last resort. You must maintain standards and hold your team accountable. Executing it correctly takes effort, though it's not something you necessarily hope to have a lot of practice doing.

Set the Right Environment: If possible, always pick a time when guests are not in the building and preferably before other staff members arrive. You should also select an open location for this meeting, something low profile and near the front door. Patios are always a solid choice. Confined spaces, like managerial offices, are not. The right location allows the team member who is receiving the unfortunate news not to feel trapped or physically stuck. If you do have to meet in a small or confined space, let the staff member sit nearest to the door.

Have a Witness: As discussed in "Witness Protection" (Chapter 13), you must have a witness for terminations, and you should also make sure to select someone whom the staff member will consider supportive, if not unbiased. This person should be another manager. If possible, avoid witnesses who also have a history of addressing negative performance with the team member.

If you require that the staff member be escorted from the restaurant, have your witness take this action, not you. You just told them they no longer work there, so they are not going to appreciate spending even more time with you as they gather their things.

On the way out, the witness should not engage in discussing reasons why the person has been let go or attempt to justify it. The witness is simply present to make sure the staff member has collected belongings and exits peacefully.

The witness does not need to be right up on that person, however. This escort is not a perp-walk. This person is not a hardened criminal. The witness should drop back and observe from afar. I have seen many terminations go badly simply because the person assigned to ensure a smooth exit instead instigated problems by their hovering.

Using the Word "Fired:" This term is unnecessarily harsh, often used by managers who want to be assertive with their termination. What you want is just an amicable end. Instead of "fired" or "terminated," use "not working out," "let you go," or simply "end your employment." They will get the message.

Over-Justifying Why: You obviously need to point to the reasons for the dismissal, plus complete whatever paperwork is required by your restaurant. If the termination is based on poor performance that they have exhibited in the past, then you should have a documented history of coaching and warnings. If this is the case, you should simply state, "Todd, we have documented your tardiness on multiple occasions. The last time we spoke, I mentioned that the next infraction would likely result in your not being on staff. This morning you were 20 minutes late. This isn't working out, and I am going to let you go."

The termination is not meant to be an educational lesson for them, however. In order for people to learn anything in life, they must be in an open headspace to receive information. Once your staff members understand they are being let go, they could probably not be more closed off. At this point, just let it be what it is. **Talking Too Long:** Keep it very concise and to the point. You should limit it to a few sentences at most. Avoid asking if they have any questions, but be open to answering any that they mention. Attempt to answer as succinctly as possible. Do not elaborate. They probably have a hundred questions simply because they likely don't agree with the decision. There is nothing that you can say to make the situation better for the person, so being brief and letting them leave is the most helpful thing you can do.

Think of it like a dating relationship. If you are breaking up with someone and they don't agree that it isn't a right match, nothing you are going to say will convince them otherwise. The more questions you attempt to answer, the more it devolves into an argument with their wanting you to justify your reason. This impasse may escalate the conversation as they attempt to argue their points, which ultimately will not change your decision.

Inserting Yourself: This situation isn't about you. Don't make statements like "it was a really tough decision" or "this is difficult for me." It is much harder on them. You still have a job.

Statements like those are made by weak managers who still want the terminated individual to like them. Do not explain how anguished you were in making the call, even if it was a struggle for you. It also makes it harder for the person to accept. "If you had the opportunity to make another decision," they might wonder, "then why didn't you?"

Firing in the Moment: There is no reason for sudden termination, and it will always work against you. It does not matter if a runner deliberately throws a full tub of marinara sauce on the floor at the host stand, splashing both staff and guests (true story). You should not terminate them on the spot.

It is easy to assume when something happens publicly that it is definitely worthy of termination or that you should also respond openly as a message to your staff. Unfortunately, instant recrimination means that you are reacting instead of planning. You still need to select a witness, pick the location, and fill out the necessary paperwork before dismissing the individual.

The answer is always to send them home in the moment and schedule a time before their next shift. That way you can collect your thoughts and execute the termination properly. It also allows the staff member to compose themselves as well. This step is important as it keeps the future separation conversation as calm as possible.

Waiting Too Long: Nearly as bad as firing in the moment, in the case of ending someone's employment for a major infraction (theft, fighting, abusive behavior), you should also not over-delay. For example, if you discover a bartender giving away free drinks, you should not allow them to work additional days before removing them. You should schedule the termination at the beginning of their next shift.

The delay usually happens because managers are scrounging to find coverage on the schedule and want to make sure they are set before making the move. Not only is such delay bad form, it could likely work against you in a wrongful termination suit.

Vilifying the Departed: Do not talk about the reasons behind someone's exit or whether the termination was the result of bad behavior toward either your staff or guests. When asked, simply state, "Todd is no longer with the restaurant, and we wish him well in his future endeavors." If asked for additional explanation, continue to repeat the aforementioned statement. Your staff will likely already know why someone was let go, as they have been working alongside them.

If you disparage the former team member, your current staff will take note. If they feel you are being disrespectful in your depiction, they might assume you will act similarly toward them as well. Friends of that person might also ask in an attempt to communicate back with that person or stir support for their return (which you should never entertain). In addition, your words could be used in legal proceedings, including slander and harassment suits.

More importantly, at one point, that terminated person was a member on your team. Now, for whatever reason, you have had to part ways. When someone does not work out, it is usually because they were a bad fit for the role or were in a bad place personally. Just because they failed for you does not mean they cannot be successful in another company. Your negative words could spread beyond your restaurant and negatively affect their chances for redemption somewhere else.

There are no good reasons to vilify. This former staff member is now a potential guest. You should always treat them with the same level of respect. On the other hand, they very well might bash you, maybe to your current and former staff and possibly online. As much as you might be tempted to "clear your name," do not address in-person or online remarks whatever might have been said. Understand their disappointment and realize they see such action as their only way to continue to engage with your restaurant. They are angry, disappointed, and maybe even scared for the future. Their anger will subside in time, along with the online campaign to have your head.

THE IMPACT OF TERMINATION

Unfortunately, I have fired hundreds of people, mainly for inadequate performance. On several occasions, I terminated staff for belligerent behaviors, such as stealing, fighting, and bullying.

Early in my career, I terminated someone for skimming money. It was a clear-cut case, and I fired him confidently. No discussion required; no warnings needed. I had discovered an obvious criminal and eradicated him, quite pleased with my decisiveness. A few months later, I heard he was homeless.

Although some might perceive that outcome as justice for a thief, the image still bothers me. I never lost sight of the fact that I am the one who indirectly put him on the street, and I still think about him every time I let someone go.

I wonder if I could have done more or if I would handle it differently now. I define my failures by those people I didn't help and whose lives were not improved by my involvement. Although stealing cash is a blatant cause for termination, it is also a sign of desperation and possibly an unorthodox call for help.

I was justified in my actions, but perhaps I could have had a conversation with him first. If it were today, maybe I would have confronted him with the evidence, pinpointed his motivations, offered him the chance to change, and monitored his progress. At least I surely like to think that I would.

Surprise! Chapter Review:
12 Rules of Termination

1. Always remember you are creating a moment that they might hold onto forever.

2. Never use the terms "fired" or "terminated."

3. Always select a location that is low profile and where they're close to the door.

4. Always make sure the witness is a supportive choice for the staff member.

5. Always keep it very short.

6. Always avoid opening the discussion for too many questions.

7. Never talk about how hard the decision is for you.

8. Never treat them like criminals if you accompany them to get their belongings.

9. Always remember that your former staff member is now a potential guest and deserves the same respect.

10. Never fire in the moment.

11. Never allow them to work another shift before terminating for cause.

12. Never discuss with anyone else the reasons someone was let go.

Bottom Line: By selecting the right environment and being concise in your communication, you will have the best chance of delivering a supportive, drama-free termination.

CHAPTER 14

UPGRADING YOUR "TABLE TOUCH"

Every night you ask the guests at each table, "How is everything?" Their answers are always positive. *Surprise!* Your online review scores begin to plummet, and your return rate is dwindling. What should you do?

Quality table touching is difficult. It is the equivalent of hosting a party where you don't know anyone and are asked to make small talk with every person there. When managers tell me how much they love talking to guests, I know it's an exaggeration. Very few naturally excel at it. You are required to find graceful ways to insert yourself, mindful not to interrupt existing conversations, and not overstay your welcome.

Unfortunately, if you do not make an attempt to connect with every guest, you will miss the opportunity to improve experiences as well as lose out on feedback about menu and service necessary to improve your venue.

Most restaurants require a 100-percent table touch. Although the exact opportunity might vary, the best time is between the delivery of the main course and the subsequent clearing of the table. You are attempting to gather information from your guests, some of whom don't want you to interrupt. Because of this awkward balance, many managers deliver what I call the "lazy touch."

THE "LAZY TOUCH" APPROACH

The lazy touch is when a manager walks from one table to another, barely slowing down, not really making eye contact, and asking the exact same question, "How's everything?"

Certainly, you have experienced this treatment hundreds of times when you have gone out to eat. Some low-energy manager shuffles their way methodically to every group, blurting out that same two-word question. The response is usually fake nods and half-smiles from guests with mouths full of food.

This lazy touch manager is not asking because they crave information; they are doing so because their job mandates table touching. That way, when asked by their boss, they can say, "Yep, I talked to everyone."

This apathetic activity yields no better result than had they simply poked the table with their finger. In my experience, most restaurant managers unfortunately embrace the lazy touch over the more difficult quality approach.

THE QUALITY APPROACH

The following are ways to promote genuine guest communication and elicit maximum feedback:

Ask directed questions: Instead of addressing the group with broad inquiries, pinpoint specific items and ask individually. Pay attention to their menu choice. Consider the difference between "How are you liking everything?" versus "May I ask your feedback on our truffle gnocchi?" Focus on those dishes that are either new to the menu or that you have struggled to perfect, stating, "We are working on a new recipe for this item and would love your thoughts."

Don't start off by apologizing: You have just interrupted their experience, so you are naturally tempted to state, "Sorry for my interruption." Fight that urge. Starting a conversation with an apology immediately makes your presence feel like an imposition. Apologies are meant for something you regret. You should not feel bad about inquiring about their visit. You are asking genuine questions to improve your business.

If you do find yourself feeling apologetic, replace "Sorry for my interruption" with "I wanted to quickly thank you all for being here tonight." After they acknowledge your genuine outreach, you can lead into "May I ask for your feedback on our..." and proceed from there in a conversational manner.

Replace "the" with "our:" Although subtle, there is a difference between "May I ask your thoughts about *the* shrimp tacos" verses "May I ask your thoughts about *our* shrimp tacos." The first one sounds like you are initiating a conversation about a disconnected third party, as if the two of you were going to weigh in on your opinions together. Using "our" assigns ownership. You are asking about a specific dish because it is yours and thus are invested in genuine feedback.

Avoid inquiries with one-word answers: Asking "How do you like our salmon?" allows the guest the opportunity to provide a short, uninformative response: "It's good" or "I like it." Instead, you should always pose your questions so they cannot be easily dismissed. Using statements such as "I would appreciate your feedback on..." or "May I ask your opinion of..." will usually provide more comprehensive replies. Getting such details is an essential tactic to locate people more or less likely to provide negative comments.

Zigzag: Your guest communication must appear sincere. Nothing will diminish this fact more than touching tables sequentially. Your arrival should be natural and well-timed, not as part of a sequence. Savvy diners will recognize the table-to-table approach, determining you are engaging them merely as a chore. Once you make contact with one table, go help run food or check the restrooms. Do anything that removes you from the floor so that when you return to talk to other guests, it is purposeful.

Read the table: As much as you know that 100-percent touches are necessary, be aware of guests who definitely do not want to be approached. Whether they are lawyers buried in their laptops, bickering spouses, or a boisterous family gathering engaged in multiple conversations at the same time, your presence is not necessarily always welcome. This foreknowledge does not mean you shouldn't interact, however.

If you cannot insert yourself in the conversation gracefully, find ways to support service. Help deliver their meal and then introduce yourself by saying something like, "I am Todd, the manager, and I'll be back to check shortly to make sure everything is exceptional." That way, they know you are returning. Pre-bussing dishes is also an easy way to connect. As you are clearing, if there is a lull in their discussion, you can naturally ask for feedback. Don't let difficult introductions deter you from gathering vital information.

Ask because you really want to know: Finally, you should be table touching because you are invested in the success of the restaurant and truly want to collect data to help grow. You must be appreciative of those who communicate and want to know their thoughts. This dynamic is the backbone of hospitality. Think of it as hosting a house party, attended by people you have never met. If you are not comfortable striking up conversations 50 times a day, every single day, then you will never find success in this industry.

Surprise! Chapter Review:
Seven Rules to Touching Tables Properly

1. Always ask directed questions. Vague inquiries will only elicit general answers.

2. Never start by apologizing. There is a reason you are asking.

3. Always use the term "our." It shows ownership and a desire to learn.

4. Never accept one-word feedback, which is only designed to make you leave. Have another question ready in such cases.

5. Always vary your visit around the dining room, not sequentially from one table to the next. Your interactions need to appear to be deliberate, not robotic.

6. Always read the table. Forcing your way into a conversation will never equal hospitality.

7. Always ask because you really want to know.

Bottom Line: Gathering information from every guest is the only way to improve your restaurant. The key to mastering table touching is first admitting you likely find it to be challenging, then adopt new techniques and verbiage to make it easier.

CHAPTER 15

HOW TO FIX A "BROKEN" TABLE

You have a rule: Anyone who complains gets a free dessert. On your follow-ups, you find that only some guests truly appreciate the gesture. *Surprise!* Many are underwhelmed by the response. What should you do?

In the restaurant business, there are three types of commenters. You encounter all three on a daily basis. You'll surely recognize yourself as one of them.

THE INTROVERTED COMMENTER

When is the last time you spoke up at a restaurant about your meal? If you are like I am, such occasions are very few and far between. I reserve this action only if something is completely inedible: raw chicken breasts, frozen fish filets, or even something like multiple fingernails (yes, I have eaten around a single nail to avoid bringing attention to my table).

I do not want a long manager interaction or a big apology. I just want edible food, and I want to pay for it. I am an **introverted commenter**.

THE EXTROVERTED COMMENTER

The opposite is an **extroverted commenter**. This guest is someone who is completely at ease providing feedback on meals that do not meet their expectations, whether prepared to recipe or not. Extroverted commenters are also more likely to highlight other perceived deficit areas, such as interactions with staff, lighting choices, music selection, etc.

This type of guest is also prone to leaving negative reviews on social media if their concerns are not addressed in the moment. Furthermore, they appreciate the attention at the table from management, as well as the attempts to provide discounts to their bill.

The extroverted commenter is often mislabeled as an annoyance—someone who enjoys complaining or is angling for a comp meal.

As a restaurant manager, you should value those who are willing to let you know their opinions. How else are you going to know where you can improve? It also gives you an opportunity to build a relationship with this guest. When people feel they have been heard, they have a positive experience regardless of what they perceived was not up to par.

THE NON-COMMENTER

The third and most elusive category is the **non-commenter**. These guests say almost nothing. You can ask them about their visit, and they provide monosyllabic responses like "fine" and "good." If you press for more information, they will give further reassurances that everything is okay.

Non-commenters are essential to locate and are often hidden like Easter eggs throughout your restaurant. They do not alert anyone to their displeasure and are most likely to *quietly* never return.

The key to deciphering that type of guest is focusing on what is not said and what is not eaten. "Fine" is not "delicious;"

"good" is not "glorious." The non-commenter is not trying to be evasive, they are just underwhelmed and answer with bland responses that mirror their experience. Coupled with a half-eaten meal, they are telling you their opinion without actually stating it. If you are not touching tables, you will never appease non-commenters. Like in many other areas of life, nonverbal communication may be louder than verbal.

KNOWING HOW TO RECOVER

Once you have uncovered a disappointed guest, how do you rectify?

Although the common response is sending a complimentary drink or dessert, blanket solutions cannot resolve all issues. The introverted commenter could be uncomfortable with the gesture, the extroverted commenter might not feel it satisfactorily addresses their concerns, and the non-commenter could go either way. There are also varying degrees of dissatisfaction, so you must determine the proper response case-by-case.

You now have a broken table on your hands. How do you fix it?

Step 1: Determine the type of commenter they are: Examine how you came across their dissatisfaction. Did they speak up only when asked, or did they volunteer their thoughts without prompting? How much are they saying? Is it just a few words or a few paragraphs? What about their body language? Are they making eye contact or are they looking down while explaining the issue? Are they making big arm gestures or maybe clinching their hands together tightly?

Step 2: Determine the severity of their discontent: Beyond a guest blatantly screaming, "This sucks! I'm not paying for this," the best determiner is: Are they still eating the meal or have they pushed it away? Their willingness to continue consuming the dish after commenting shows the level of displeasure; requesting the plate to be removed shows disgust. The latter requires an immediate solution, as they are sitting hungry while others at the table are eating, or, in some cases, have stopped as well in solidarity.

Growing up, most of us had the same rule at the dinner table: Nobody eats until everyone has a full plate in front of them. In many families, this practice extends to restaurant visits. If the server forgot my sister's meal, everybody at the table would wait until she received her fettucine alfredo. Intended to be polite to the person excluded, it comes with the side effect of making everyone else's meal cold. That forgotten pasta doesn't just influence one person but the entire group.

Such mistakes are why you must gauge the frustration level of *everyone* at the table. Sometimes, an introverted diner might discreetly point out an issue but their friend is the one rolling their eyes. When you notice those actions, you must modify your resolution to include everyone. Instead of a slice of pie for the one whose food was late, maybe everything on the dessert menu arrives at their table. That way everyone who was affected is being recognized for the inconvenience.

Step 3: Do not defend: If a guest says the 16-ounce steak sandwich is too small, don't give into the temptation to reply, "You know that's a full pound of meat there, correct?" Your instinct to protect the restaurant is admirable, but your defensiveness will never provide satisfaction. Your goal should never be to convince people they are wrong.

I have had guests cut into their chicken, release a small amount of blood, and become convinced we served them raw food. Although the chicken is thoroughly cooked, and the guest is mistaken, good luck attempting to explain why the chicken is fully cooked. I actually did try a few times. "I know you see pink there, but this is a natural occurrence with any cut closer to the darker meat like wings, legs, thighs. Actually, the fact that this happened shows that we don't overcook our chickens."

This tactic worked zero percent of the time. It's hard to convince someone to eat what the person thinks is undercooked meat, even though it isn't undercooked. In this case, I would simply apologize and offer to replace it with our lasagna.

Another point to keep in mind when these situations arise is that it can be challenging to know the appropriate amount to discount. An insufficient gesture will result in negative feelings. On the flipside, it is easy to give away the house if it is not your money. Keep a log of your comps, including the detailed reasons for each, and periodically review with other managers and owners. This comparison should let you know if you are offering too much or too little.

In the meantime, the key to avoiding large discounts is uncovering issues *before* they are brought to your attention. If the kitchen is dragging 20 minutes on table 12, then you must address those guests within 10 minutes to let them know. When you notice your servers in the weeds, you need to talk with their guests to determine if service has suffered. If you notice people not loving their meals, simply have a conversation with them and learn how you can become better.

As long as you continue to avoid the "Lazy Touch," you won't need to give away free things as often to prompt the guests to return. They will do so because they appreciate your willingness to listen and your genuine desire to improve.

Surprise! Chapter Review:
Five Rules for a Successful Table Recovery

1. Decide which type of commenter they are. This determination will dictate how much of you they really want at their table.

2. Determine the level of severity of their displeasure. This observation will help you to decide the appropriate response.

3. Never get defensive. Allow the guest to vent. Being heard matters.

4. Always apologize. Even if it is not your fault, take ownership. This tactic is the best way to diffuse a guest issue.

5. Do not bargain comp. When in doubt, discount more. Better to overshoot than underwhelm.

Bottom Line: Determining which of the three types of commenters you are encountering provides a better roadmap for guest recovery and knowing the compensation level to extend.

CHAPTER 16

CONQUERING ONLINE REVIEWS

You answer every negative online review publicly, letting anyone who visits the site know that you are addressing all issues. Your replies are straightforward, admitting fault on occasion and defending your restaurant appropriately when applicable. *Surprise!* Your posts rarely receive any responses from your outreach and your star rating is dropping. What should you do?

Let me just put my view out there: I don't like Yelp. Actually, I dislike all platforms that allow negative online feedback about my businesses.

It's ridiculous to spend all my time locating, planning, staffing, training, and launching a place only to have some anonymous clown post "Didn't like the wallpaper...1 star." It feels malicious and unjust, and from people who likely have no idea how hard it is to open a restaurant.

This situation then begs a very significant question: why should any manager care about online reviews?

For example, I opened a barbeque place with a few partners. The place was an earnest attempt to replicate our mutual love for southern cuisine. BBQ is personal, particularly because nearly everyone has attempted it in their backyards and thinks they know the perfect method. You don't hear people leaving Japanese restaurants saying, "I could make better sushi at home!" That reaction is not the same for ribs.

Although we did receive some solid praise, others seemed to have hated us. Looking back now, there are things I would have done differently, but that venture resulted in some of the most vitriolic reviews I have received before or since. There was even a thread on one site called *"I Feel So Ripped and Dissed,"* which details one guest's dissatisfaction with their visit, followed by 37 other people responding with similar disdain.

Back then, I took these comments quite personally and was unable to separate my emotions. I was angry and defensive, deciding it was ultimately the reviewers who had the problem. I finally realized I was focusing on defending my business, and my own ego, instead of listening to the guest's level of disappointment. This experience became the catalyst for developing a better strategy for responding to online feedback.

ABANDONING YOUR DESIRE FOR FAIRNESS

In another instance, I had a review at another restaurant where the guest didn't care for the fried chicken because of the inclusion of the leafy garnish. To be clear, it was so inconsequential that it usually blew off the plate while running it to the table.

It would be easy to dismiss this reviewer as a fool. The sprig had no bearing on the dish whatsoever, but the natural tendency to be correct is the exact thing you cannot focus on when addressing reviews. You will never convince the reviewer that they were wrong.

Now take a look at this actual review:

"You can definitely skip this place. This issue is not the cost (yes, it is pricey) but the dismal food. The food is tasteless, bland, and genuinely unappealing. A Swanson's TV dinner from a microwave would be a considerable step up. They should add McDonald's to the menu (burgers, fries, and shakes) so that guests will have something to eat."

Sounds terrible, right? The review is actually about one of the most celebrated 3-Star Michelin restaurants on the planet. It is safe to say that the reviewer is wrong, at least in the minds of the vast majority of the culinary world. But trying to convince this person of anything different will fail.

The key here is to understand that it is not about being right.

The reason for posting these comments is not about the garnish or, in the case of the Michelin restaurant review, the need for McDonald's on the menu. It's a small indicator of a much greater issue: Disappointment. These guests were looking forward to a remarkable experience but, in their minds, they were left to feel unimpressed and insignificant.

TARGETING A GUEST'S MOTIVATIONS

As a restaurant manager, you should live by the mantra "No one should ever have to pay for something they did not like."

Asking a guest to do so makes them feel, well, "ripped and dissed." If you encounter someone who is not satisfied, it's better to comp the dish on the spot than to attempt to recover their experience later. That's what the vast majority of negative online reviews are: people who feel shortchanged and still care enough to write about their visit.

Who writes these reviews? With limited variation, the profile of a typical reviewer follows a pattern.

First, they are convinced their opinions are facts. No room for disagreement.

Second, they believe they have a unique talent for assessing restaurants, likely viewing themselves as a "foodie."

And, lastly, they feel it is their duty to communicate their opinions. They believe they have an audience and an obligation to warn them about a restaurant, or in some cases, celebrate it.

REVIEWS ARE NOT MEANT FOR YOU

The common denominator in every review is that they are

never written to the business itself. An example might be: "We showed up for our reservation to find that our table wasn't ready. Once we were seated, our pork was cold and the drinks were warm. Not worth it." The intended audience for every review is the public and specifically potential future patrons.

Therefore, there is a very important strategy for addressing negative reviews. When you reach out, you must thank them for their feedback as though their review is directed to the business. An opening sentence might be: "I appreciate you reaching out to us about your recent visit."

This response is meant to get the reviewer off their soapbox and create a one-on-one dialogue. Once you have established this private communication, you can begin the recovery.

Think of the energy it takes to write a negative review. Examine it in terms of a romantic relationship. As long as there is a discourse, whether positive or negative, there is passion. It is only when apathy emerges that the connection is gone. Acknowledging that this person was disappointed, yet passionate enough to craft a critique, you should actually appreciate their negative review.

After all, **if it weren't for their online feedback, you would not have the opportunity to address an inferior experience.** Without this communication, you would ultimately experience a decline in guests and decrease in sales.

Your concern is not the guest who writes a 1-star review. You should be worried about the ones who silently leave and never return.

KEYS TO SUCCESSFUL RECOVERY

There are a few simple guidelines you can follow when it comes to negative reviews.

When you make contact, do so privately: This stems from the reviewer's tendency to address the public, instead of your restaurant. If you respond likewise, it will only make the reviewer think you are more concerned about public perception than addressing their recent experience. If a platform does not allow you to reach out privately, post a simple reply with your email requesting for them to email you with additional feedback.

When you reach out, write each response from scratch: If you are currently using a template, delete it immediately. Writing each response individually will require you to truly examine their concerns first and provide a genuine reply. Also, occasionally multiple guests at the same table will write reviews. If you send the exact same response to all, they will compare notes and probably consider your gesture to be disingenuous. Finally, write your response expecting it to be publicly posted by the commenter because that likelihood is a real possibility.

Welcome them back as your guest: You will not get people to change their mind without them having a better visit in your restaurant. You must invite them to come back. Ask them to bring a friend and definitely reassure them that there will not be a charge. Let them know you will be handling their reservation personally.

When they do return, make sure you are in the building so you can chat with them, though avoid doing so at the beginning of the meal. Otherwise, they think you have carefully orchestrated every aspect to ensure success—even though you definitely have. Remember, they likely consider themselves as a kind of food critic who wants to judge your restaurant again "fairly."

Think of this return guest like you would an actual restaurant critic. If they determine you have spotted them, they automatically assume that their experience has been modified in some way. When that situation happens, a professional critic cannot get a handle on what normal guests encounter, which doesn't work for their audience.

Avoid the temptation to "play detective:" You might think the reviewers are fake and just want something for free. Yes, there are people who post criticism in an attempt to abuse your kindness, but they are the vast minority. If you are trying to determine the validity of every review, you are disregarding some useful information and losing out on a needed recovery. It also means you are focused on the wrong percentage.

Playing detective is not only a waste of energy, it can easily punish legitimate reviewers. The more you attempt to uncover those few trying to take advantage, the greater the likelihood that you will incorrectly dismiss actual feedback. It also makes responding to the reviews adversarial, which it does not need to be.

Assume that a very small percentage are attempting to game the system. Giving them a free meal is the cost of doing business. Focus on the vast majority who were disappointed with their experience and deserve better.

When you contact, never ask them to change their review: Don't even mention the rating. You invite them back to prove that you can do better. Once you make this gesture, they will usually update their review on their own. If you make it all about the score, they will feel that factor is your sole motivation. If they haven't posted an updated review within a week after the return visit, a follow-up email thanking them for the opportunity to provide them a better experience should prompt their change of heart. No guarantees, though.

EXAMPLE OF A REVIEW AND RESPONSE

The following is a basic review and my typical response.

REVIEW:

From Amy W: I went on a Saturday night. My reservation was at 7:00 but they didn't get my table ready until 7:15. Strike 1. Our Caesar salad was great, but I thought the crab cakes were burnt. We also didn't like the lobster mac & cheese. Tasted like Velveeta. Strike 2. When I asked our waiter for mayo for the crab cakes, he rolled his eyes. You can tell he didn't want us there. Strike 3. This place looks good but there are a lot better in the neighborhood.

RESPONSE:

Dear Amy:

Thank you so much for reaching out to us. It is only through honest feedback that we have the opportunity to improve, and based on your visit we have a lot of work to do.

My apologies for the delay in seating. I will work with the host team on better pacing our reservations. I have also shared your comments about the crab cake and lobster dish with our culinary team. Also, the attitude you received from your server is unacceptable. We strive to provide excellent hospitality, and what you experienced is anything but hospitable.

Most importantly, a manager should have been at your table making sure everything was exceptional. For this and everything else, I truly apologize.

I know we can do better and would appreciate the opportunity to show you. If you are willing, please come back. Bring a friend, and you both will be my guest. I will personally take care of all the arrangements, and there will be no charge.

I guarantee that your next visit will far exceed your previous one. Please reach out to me on my cell at _____ or via email at _____. I look forward to hearing from you soon.

Sincerely,

Ken McGarrie, Restaurant Manager

DON'T GHOSTWRITE YOUR OWN REVIEWS

As much as you might want to attempt filling review sites with self-created content, don't. Not only will this deception reduce your motivation solely to a star rating—instead of improving your restaurant—but your account will likely get locked out.

Review sites are on high alert and look for denominators that appear to be fraud (multiple postings within a short time frame, all positive reviews, same IP addresses). Once their automated bots consider your page to be in violation, the majority of your positive reviews will be suppressed or removed.

I have known several owners who asked everyone at their grand openings to go on Yelp and say great things. The mass influx of all positive reviews within a short time frame flagged their accounts. Soon all the 5-star posts were "unrecommended," and the only reviews left were negative.

Avoid the temptation. Just use the sites for what they are intended, reconnecting with guests who have strong opinions about your restaurant.

POSITIVE REVIEWS

Similarly, you also should respond to the positive reviews with the same sincerity as with the negative ones. Again, write from scratch, with the offer of providing them something extra on their return visit. Not only does it reinforce their good feelings about your restaurant, it also makes you feel better to connect with people who love what you do. The effect will help curb the tendency to read countless 5-star reviews but obsess solely on a single 1-star outlier.

If you only focus on the poor comments, you will miss the celebration of the compliments. Make sure that the positive feedback is ringing as loudly for you as the negative and with equal frequency. It is good for the soul.

Review sites are useful tools for restaurants, allowing us the opportunity to catch those guests who left dissatisfied. It is a table touch beyond the four walls of the venue. Although I still don't like Yelp, I guess I am ultimately thankful for it.

Surprise! Chapter Review:
Eight Rules to Repairing Negative Reviews

1. Always reach out privately (if possible). If not, post your email and request a private chat.

2. Never defend your restaurant. It is not about being right.

3. Never use a form letter. That format comes across as obvious and stale.

4. Always thank them for reaching out to you and acknowledge that their feedback helps you to improve.

5. Always apologize for any negative experience. Do not mention any positive aspects they might have mentioned.

6. Always ask them to return as your guest. Let them know it will be free.

7. Never mention the star rating. It equates to being only about your score and reduces the perception about why you are reaching out.

8. Never ask them to change their original comments.

Bottom Line: The key to changing your online rating is not focusing on being right. Rather, addressing the reviewer's feeling of disappointment is key to turning around their opinion.

CHAPTER 17

TAKING THE SECOND STEP

The more negativity you encounter, the more stress you feel about your job. *Surprise!* You find yourself having less patience with upset guests and disgruntled staff. What should you do?

As with many professions, you will experience pressure as a restaurant manager. It can complicate your job and take you to places you don't want to go.

You already know that each table is its own ticking time bomb. You must constantly monitor the performance of every staff member to avoid an explosion. You forego dinners with your family so you can provide meals to others, spending the hours in between tackling piles of administrative tasks (scheduling, invoicing, reporting, and so on) that keep the restaurant open.

Whereas many staff members view restaurant work as a stepping-stone, you have chosen this industry as a career. Are you now finding it hard to maintain positivity in this environment? Whether from an irate guest, a dissatisfied staff member, or an irritated boss, you will encounter minefields of aggression. Your challenge is to redirect any negative energy, which is nearly impossible if you choose to process it on equal terms.

DODGING ALL PUNCHES

In martial arts, students are taught not to absorb punches but to step aside. Doing so uses exertion to their advantage. This maneuver will push the aggressor to overextend their attack, leaving them vulnerably off balance. (At least it's what I think is the training method from watching countless '80s karate movies.)

The same strategy can be repurposed to deal with animosity, by taking steps back and using others' negative efforts to your advantage. It is the difference between accepting people at face value versus understanding the reasons behind their actions.

When a guest is agitated, for instance, managers often engage solely on a surface level. Let's say that they are making quite a scene about their steak, proclaiming, "This is the worst piece of meat I've ever had! I wouldn't feed it to my dog!"

Your immediate thoughts are likely, "Is the steak that bad? Is this person wrong? Do they even have a dog?"

Although your subsequent investigation might show the steak was perfect, it is irrelevant regarding your communication with the guest. You are required to make sure they leave happy. As a manager, you must acknowledge their opinion and apologize, even though they are completely wrong and acted like a jerk. Translation: they get a free dessert, and you are at the table saying sorry for a meal that was prepared correctly.

Over time, these experiences can get on your nerves, especially if you are focusing on how unfair it all seems.

You are never going to change the behavior of others, only the way you allow them to affect you.

TAKING ONE STEP BACK

In a moment of frustration and anger, if you were to take a single step back from the situation, you would begin to see *why* a guest might act so obnoxiously. This dinner could have been an important client meeting and they were nervous it wasn't going well. Perhaps, they were having buyer's remorse about the cost.

It is rarely about the unpleasant complaint, rather the lack of control they feel in the situation. When you take one step back, you don't focus on the surface aggression as much as see the disappointment that lies beneath.

You might already employ this technique as a way to understand the why behind negativity. Unfortunately, this process does little to help you personally deal with the impact it has on your psyche. You understand that the reaction from the upset guest is not about the steak but underlying factors, such as the meal being an important occasion, sticker shock, or whatever the true reason is for their anger. At least you are managing your reaction by considering their motivations and not in a manner that evokes sympathy.

TAKING TWO STEPS BACK

The key to not allowing their negativity to affect you is found in taking two steps back. Now that you have determined that their antagonism is based in disappointment, then you must work to examine the connected emotion. The reason for making such a scene is always rooted in insecurity, such as them being irrationally convinced that they are somehow being singled out for a bad steak. It is likely a pattern in their life, employing hostility to mask their own self-doubt, but those managers willing to look even deeper will see only the guest's fright and uncertainty.

Taking two steps back reveals a person's vulnerability, providing you with the best and only rational response: compassion.

STEPPING BACK PUT INTO PRACTICE

Stepping Back with Your Guests: The next time you encounter a guest yelling about how their server is purposely ignoring them, consider how insecure they must be to come to this conclusion. Your frustration with the conversation will instinctively be replaced with pity. You will still have to gratuitously apologize, but since you are viewing the exchange with compas-

sion, you won't internalize negative feelings about it.
Stepping Back with Your Team: This method works with
staff aggression as well. Managing concerns can take a toll if you
are unable to process the information and provide clear-minded
responses. Take the example of server Todd claiming he is not being
assigned tables in proper rotation. I am sure you have encountered that one. Todd can be quite frustrating. There he is in the
middle of service, telling you, "The schedule is unfair, and the
hosts are intentionally not seating me." You know full well that
he is not maliciously being skipped and doubt that the rotation
is unbalanced.

Your surface-level response is probably to defend the hosts
and yourself. "That is not true," you might respond. "I do the
schedule and make sure everyone gets equal shifts. Also, if you
look at the reservations, you will see that you are being seated in
rotation." In this case, you are taking his negativity and meeting
it with equal hostility. Your message to Todd here is defensive
and dismissive—and ultimately ineffective.

Now take a single step back and hear his complaint again. It
changes from the "everything sucks" tone to what his words are
actually saying: "I am not making the money I need to pay bills.
I also don't think the hosts like me."

After understanding the *why* behind the comments, your approach to Todd may resemble: "I will see what I can do to get
you more shifts to help you out. Also, I am sure the hosts really
like you. You are a very enjoyable person."

That redress might feel like a supportive response, but it is actually also quite ineffectual. In an attempt to make him happier,
you have now taken on the responsibility of being the nurturer.

I know a lot of managers who refer to themselves as the mom/
dad/psychiatrist of the restaurant and don't see anything wrong
with it. Unfortunately, being the comforting type is a burden.
Surely, staff members deserve reassurance on occasion. Best to
think of that role like a clock you have to wind, however. If it
needs to happen once a month, so be it. But if you have to tend

to it every three days, it becomes laborious. Your staff represents dozens of clocks, and the easiest way to spend every day winding them is to provide saccharine responses to their concerns.

Now, listen to Todd's concerns from two steps back. His message morphs from "unfair" to "nobody likes me" to finally: "I am afraid I might not be good enough, and I fear it is my fault that people don't like me."

Now that you are addressing his truth, you can do so with empathy. You are mindful to focus on productivity, not coddling, and offer a truly valuable response: "Your performance is valued tremendously by your coworkers and the management team. Let's both monitor the server schedule and rotation and plan a follow-up one week from today to discuss the data we will have collected."

You are reassuring Todd of his value but have avoided the nurturer role by not addressing it with reassuring words only. You are requesting data instead of relying on opinion. This approach allows you to keep your own emotion out of the equation, which exists at the surface level. It should also help to get you out of the parenting mindset, which is mentally exhausting.

The farther back you go, the better view you will have to calculate the proper communication. Now the initial concern based on opinion is met with the second-level response of providing performance feedback and establishing a plan to gather facts. You understand that the staff member does not have ill intent, which allows you to respond productively. It is managing your response instead of someone else doing so.

Stepping Back with Your Boss: Not only does this method work for guests and staff, it is nearly essential when interacting with bosses. The next time you hear your employer rant about underwhelming sales, consider the steps. They likely took on investors to fund the restaurant with the promise of solid returns. Also, they are no more equipped with the solution to increase sales than you are or they would have acted upon this strategy already. It is this inability to rectify the situation that makes them feel vulnerable.

Upon taking a step back, their initial rant to you of "our sales are garbage, and no one here is doing enough to fix it!" suddenly becomes: "I thought this business was going to work out better. I promised our investors a 12 percent ROI." And then with two steps back, it becomes: "I don't know how to fix this, and I am scared I might not be able to succeed."

Now you can see bosses for the fears and insecurities they possess, same as you. It doesn't rectify sales, but it does make you more empathetic when their frustrations become evident.

Stepping Back with Yourself: The next time you hear yourself screaming in traffic, consider the reason. I guarantee you that it isn't the car in front of you that has triggered your stream of obscenities. You are angry about something entirely different, but you have allowed it to manifest into pointless road rage.

Acknowledge that your hostility is merely an attempt to distract yourself from your own fear and insecurities. Be willing to tackle the true issues making you anxious. Also, in the same way you will need to forgive the aggressive guest or the hotheaded boss, make sure to forgive yourself for acting like a complete jerk. Hopefully, the car you flipped off will do the same.

This tactic is by no means simple, and in the heat of the moment, it is easy to slip back into face-value reactions. Nobody is able to remain two steps back in every situation, and it takes practice and patience to master. Once you regularly employ this practice, your stress level will decrease. As long as you can see people for who they truly are, their aggression will not get to you to make you dislike your job.

Surprise! Chapter Review:
Worst-to-Best Stress-Coping Mechanisms

- **Surface**: Meeting anger with equal aggression.

  <u>Stress Level</u>: High. You are guaranteed to internalize negativity.

- **One Step Back**: Seeking the "why" behind other people's reactions.

  <u>Stress Level:</u> Medium. Getting to the root cause of their negativity will put their behavior in a more understandable light, although you are still taking on the stress.

- **Two Steps Back**: Viewing extreme anger and negativity with the pity it deserves.

  <u>Stress Level:</u> Low. Focusing on how hostility is rooted in insecurity and feeling out of control, you are left to only view their actions with compassion. This practice will also alleviate the stress you take upon yourself.

Bottom Line: You will never be able to manage how others communicate, only the extent to which you internalize their aggression.

CHAPTER 18

EMBRACING BLUNT CRITICISM

You like it when people are kind and communicate without intensity. You equate strong opinions with hostility and have no appreciation for those who speak curtly and aggressively, including your boss. *Surprise!* You find yourself on the outs with those same people who provide blunt criticism. What should you do?

Let's face it, most people are incapable of appreciating direct feedback. Accepting truth requires being open to suggestions and looking beyond mere words to focus on the positive intentions behind them. The messenger often has your interests in mind, and ignoring their comments comes at your own peril. I learned this outcome the hard way on the subject of smoking at work.

IGNORING GOOD ADVICE

I worked at a catering company when I was 19. I mostly remember the mushroom caps. They were unusually popular so we prepped a ton of them. There was really no method to what the "stuffing" was—usually a mixture of the proteins and vegetables closest to expiring that we found in the walk-in. During holidays, the pace was especially excruciating, with some staff opting to sleep in the restaurant between shifts.

That job was where I learned to eat meals standing over a trash can. It is also where I learned the sole advantage of smoking. The only time it was acceptable to leave my post was for a cigarette.

The habit followed me for years. Although I had long moved into management, I could still be found huddled behind dumpsters. A quick hand wash and a mint and I thought I was ready to touch tables. It wasn't until a run-in with an investor that I learned the professional ramifications of smoking.

He was a person who owned multiple successful corporations and didn't waste energy on being chatty. He once summed up a site visit in the only three words he spoke to me that day: "Poop on toilet." Though he didn't say "poop." I expected people to be welcoming and friendly, but he was neither. He was honest and direct. I did not like this guy. So when he told me bluntly that I "smelled like an ashtray," I wasn't in the place where I could hear the message. I was too busy being a hater to acknowledge that he had a valid point.

The investor was actually doing me a favor by being straightforward. If you have a boss who is honest in their opinions, learn to embrace the honesty. Too many leaders have a tendency to sugarcoat their criticism, dancing around their concerns about your performance or habits, instead of providing clear direction. Obviously, there is a balance between "everything is terrific" and "poop on toilet," but given the option, be brave enough to work for those who speak their minds.

Consider the criticisms that bother you the most. What you rage against in others is rooted in your own deepest fears. If I receive a negative review on food, I am rarely fazed. I obviously pass the comments along to the kitchen, but I am secure in the knowledge that I work with incredible culinary leaders.

In contrast, I have found myself at times indignant and defensive when challenged about service. "There's no way Amy was rude to the table," I would exclaim defensively. "She's one of our best!"

Welcoming hospitality is what I personally value most in restaurants and so it is my greatest area of concern. It is human nature to overcompensate or overreact in an attempt to mask our own insecurities, but acknowledging that tendency will help to minimize its frequency.

I understand now that my anger toward this investor was really disappointment in myself and a healthy dose of jealousy. We were the same age, yet he was a self-made multimillionaire. My only recourse was to conclude he was mean and, therefore, deserving of my contempt. When he acknowledged my stale smoke smell, it should have been a wake-up call. Deep down I knew he was right, but I let my hater-mentality get the better of me. My reaction was a lack of confidence and blinding defensiveness rearing its ugly head. When I lost that job months later, it was that same insecurity that was my undoing.

PROVIDING FEEDBACK
TO YOUR TEAM

You must always provide direct feedback to your team. The message does not necessarily need to be blunt, but it should be honest. Walking on eggshells with your staff does not spare their feelings. Instead, it creates an environment where you are focused more on their response than on the data you've gathered.

I often remind my team "We hire adults and treat you as such." I even mention it sometimes in the job posting (Chapter 6 *"Finding Great Staff"*). In turn, the expectation is that I will not need to babysit. If I have to continually track whether someone is late or not carrying their wine key, that habit is monitoring them like children.

The intent is also to establish that we will have straightforward "adult" conversations. If you have a server who is incapable of handling a full section, you obviously should give them fewer tables. You also must openly address such a decision with them. Most importantly, you need to provide steps that the server can take in order to achieve full competency. Such assistance is the part that many managers miss. It is correct to be honest with a staff member if they are not keeping up with the pack, but it's supportive to provide them with measurable actions they can take to improve.

Learn to appreciate those who are willing to be honest with you, digest their criticisms whenever possible, and be willing to be direct with others. Much like the factors that affect your restaurant's rating, you will only improve if you learn from your negative reviews and work to rectify your failings. Otherwise you are destined to be a 1-star manager.

SEEKING CRITICISM FROM YOUR TEAM

Think of those who are your harshest critics in your work-place. Bosses are an obvious choice, but what about your team? You likely receive criticism from people who work for you. You should establish a way for staff to provide feedback about the restaurant, such as a comment box or online form.

At times, these anonymous responses will likely call your performance into question. "Manager X only takes care of their favorites and gives the rest of us terrible sections," a typical criticism might read.

Much like the case with online reviews, your job is not to "play detective" and figure out who wrote what but instead to find out the answer to why they feel this way. Don't be defensive. Instead, embrace blunt critiques and see why others have that opinion of you.

Sometimes, staff criticism is not so direct. Such opinions are often some of your negative habits they have picked up on and bring to your attention as thinly veiled jokes.

For example, managers have a tendency to spend too much time in their office. It is a very common issue in restaurants and does not provide support for those working the floor. Staff might be feeling required to go out of their way to get assistance on the POS, and the managers are not at their tables guarding the guest experience.

So when a server knocks on your door and makes the offhand comment "I knew I would find you here," they are really saying that you are failing the staff.

The question then is: are you able to receive this feedback and work to adjust, or do you snap back with a defensive "Yeah, I have a lot of work to catch up on."

No matter the source, the more you are open to criticism, the more both you and your restaurant will grow.

Surprise! Chapter Review: Four Steps to Loving Criticism

1. Always focus on understanding "why" the feedback is being provided.

2. Never equate criticism with whether you are liked.

3. Always seek critiques from both direct and indirect sources.

4. Always be willing to provide the same honesty to others.

Bottom Line: When it comes to blunt feedback, always focus on the message, not the messenger.

CHAPTER 19

FINDING YOUR WORK/LIFE BALANCE

From the moment you walk into the restaurant, you are buried with responsibilities. Between numerous meetings, required accounting reports, and daily administrative tasks, you have hours of work before you go into service and several more after as well. In order to keep up, you have started doing some of your paperwork from home, much to the chagrin of your loved ones. *Surprise!* You don't have a life outside the restaurant. What should you do?

The most important aspect of restaurant management is not to become a statistic. Whereas the national average for divorce has been declining[1] in the US, bartenders, in particular, have the second highest rate[2] of all professions nationwide (52.7 percent). The numbers for restaurant managers are likely not far behind. I have seen so many marriages struggle due to the pressures of the position.

Food-service workers also have the highest rate[3] of illicit drug use (19.1 percent) and third highest rate of heavy alcohol use (11.8 percent) of any profession. According to the Mayo Clinic, drug addiction, also called substance use disorder, is a disease that affects a person's brain and behavior and leads to an inability to control the use of legal or illegal drugs or medication.[4] The restaurant field has the highest rate of substance abuse (16.9 percent) of any career in the US.

In addition, our industry ranks second[5] in the profession (5.7 percent among those in food-preparation and serving-related occupations) most likely to have "suicidal ideation" which is having thought about suicide within the last year. It is becoming harder to find someone in our industry who doesn't know at least one restaurant person who has taken their own life.

This industry is a challenging field. You are not having dinners with your own family because your job is to feed other families first. You are not frequenting restaurants with friends on the weekend as these are the times you are running your own. Managing a restaurant is a real sacrifice and one that does not work for everyone. If you find yourself coping with the stress by self-medicating with drugs and alcohol, please seek help immediately. We have simply lost too many great people to the statistics that plague our industry.

In addition, the restaurant field seems to take an unhealthy pride in producing workaholics. This tendency is a sure-fire recipe for burnout. If you are in your restaurant 60 hours a week and spending an additional 30 at home making schedules and answering emails, then you are never off duty.

I have watched countless talented leaders lose their joy and leave the industry due to lack of balance. So how do you achieve it? The key is making balance a priority in your life and continually working toward it no different than a commitment to going to the gym. It requires a daily resolve in order to reach your goals.

PRIORITIZE EXTRACURRICULARS

Speaking of the commitment, the first step is to remember your personal life. You must have activities outside of the restaurant in order to feel like you aren't working. If they happen to fall at the same time each week, even better. That way, it is established that you are always unavailable to work during a certain time frame.

Church, date night, and family outings are good examples. Volunteer work, hobbies, and fitness-related activities also come to mind. As mentioned in Chapter 4 ("*Why Hobbies Are Useful*"), hobbies help to create a well-rounded person. It is even one of the criteria upon which you judge others during an interview.

Extracurricular activities also give you a much needed mental break from work, provided that you aren't on your phone the entire time.

ESTABLISH RULES OF CONTACT

In order to encourage balance among all management, you should lay out a universal expectation of communication, based on urgency. These are mine for off-days:

Email: If the email is addressed to me specifically, expect a response within eight hours. However, if I am merely cc'd, then I will reply upon my return to work.

Level of urgency: Low. Someone is reaching out for an opinion or data. Nothing pressing.

Text: If you text me, expect a response within two hours. I think of the response time as "movie length." I should be able to check my phone as I settle into my seat and not be expected to respond to a text until the credits roll.

Level of urgency: Medium. Someone requires a response faster than an email would provide, likely time-sensitive.

Phone: Answer immediately. This action must be an emergency or close to one. This situation is why you can disable your text tones, but as a restaurant manager, you can never turn off your phone.

Level of urgency: High. It is very important, and only I have the necessary information.

The key here is to hold others to these urgency levels and

call them out when they abuse them. For example, if someone calls on my day-off to ask whether I think we should order more aprons in next week's linen delivery, I would kindly answer and then have a quick conversation as to why that didn't constitute an emergency.

STOP WORKING FROM HOME

Easier said than done, I know. With everything you are tackling on a daily basis, you likely cannot string five uninterrupted minutes together without someone needing a void or to pick up their tips from last night. It seems that your couch is the only place you get work done. It is also the antithesis of striving for a balanced life.

The solution is to schedule yourself "admin" blocks. These allotments should happen several times each week. Mid-afternoons are typically best as opportunities for you to step off the floor to tackle payroll, inventory, invoicing, etc., without interruption. Make sure you have another manager or floor supervisor on hand so your staff is still supported.

BROADCAST YOUR ACCOMPLISHMENTS

Much of burnout comes from the natural desire to show your employer that you are doing a good job. This pattern usually manifests itself in long hours to signal, "Hey, look I'm still here." Although it is vital that you are present during all your scheduled times, the desire to be noticed "working hard" can be exhausting. Also, if you are completing tasks from home, those hours are rarely acknowledged.

Instead, you should communicate your accomplishments to your boss frequently. There is a good chance they don't fully know the range of your achievements and this approach would serve to inform them. It doesn't have to be long—simply a bullet-point list of the tasks you have completed for the week. See Chapter 24 ("*Self-Promotion Is Self-Preservation*") for more on this strategy.

DELEGATE MORE

If your load is so heavy that you are unable to achieve balance, you have to accept help. Take an inventory of your weekly responsibilities and see if you might be able to offload any of them to others. If you say there aren't any responsibilities that you can offload, then you are likely bad at delegation.

Receiving help does not mean losing control of a duty. If you have a lead server write rough drafts of the online responses, you are still able to review them before posting. Same with staff schedules, invoice coding, guest receipt retrieval, and many other tasks. Reallocating some of your duties will allow you to focus on those assignments that solely require your management-level acumen, like financial reports, HR communication, and reviewing payroll. Further, it will substitute as training for those who might be interested in management and give them the opportunity to add credentials to move up in a business.

REDUCE STRESS DAILY

It might sound simplistic that you need to embrace a stress reliever in order to achieve balance, but its importance cannot be overstated. Beyond your scheduled weekly activities, you also must find something daily to take your mind elsewhere. I take spin classes because I know that, at about 17 minutes in, I will be gasping and struggling, unable to think about work. The effect lowers my stress. Find what works for you and schedule it accordingly.

As mentioned earlier, here's hoping that your stress reliever isn't always alcohol. Unfortunately, restaurants are custom-built for it, with late hours and "free" (or at least readily accessible, often at reduced cost) booze. We all know those who turned that closing drink into a full-blown addiction. Consider hot yoga instead.

WHY YOU ARE HERE

In Chapter 1 (*"Why Are You Running a Restaurant?"*), we addressed the need to keep your motivations in mind. Tattoo them on yourself if need be. As cliché as it sounds, you will eventually have *the* day for which you planned ahead. If you know that you joined the restaurant world in order to open your own place, then focusing on that goal should help you to weather those more difficult responsibilities throwing you off-balance. Whatever your ultimate goal is, always keep it in mind on rougher days.

You will hopefully also encounter others in the industry with similar goals and passions. Attempt to connect with other managers outside your restaurant and discuss common challenges. Perhaps, they have a method for invoicing that might save you time or an inventive solution for finding great staff. At the very least, they can relate to your struggles, and the time you spend with cohorts counts toward relieving stress.

BE A ROLE MODEL

You are setting an example for your staff on what it means and looks like to be a restaurant manager. They might be considering making this industry their career. If you are constantly hurried, working 15 hours a day with zero social life, then you are a terrible role model.

Let's face it: There aren't enough good restaurant managers around, and the only way that problem changes is by showing people that true balance can exist. You can have a family, friends, and extracurricular activities in your position. You just have to make them a priority.

It is up to you to make sure you have a good quality of life. No one else can do that for you.

Surprise! Chapter Review:
Eight Rules to Better Balance

1. Make time for predetermined weekly personal activities.

2. Prioritize day-off communication based on urgency.

3. Never work from home.

4. Let your bosses know what you are accomplishing.

5. Empower others to help you with smaller tasks.

6. Indulge in a healthy stress reliever daily.

7. Never forget why you chose this profession.

8. Set an example for future managers to follow.

Bottom Line: In order to achieve balance, you must tackle your personal life with the same energy and passion that you bring to your restaurant—or face inevitable burnout.

CHAPTER 20

THE COST OF AN AFTER-WORK DRINK

You agree to meet for drinks with several servers one night after work. You spend the evening throwing out stories and tossing back shots. It was an enjoyable evening, and you have no regrets. The following morning is a different story. *Surprise!* The servers who weren't there feel excluded and make comments about your having favorites among the staff. What should you do?

You need to make sure you're making clear distinctions when it comes to extracurricular activities. I am speaking specifically about the tendency to get drinks after work with staff or hanging out with them socially.

As much as you might be dedicated to avoiding conflict, you are likely going to find yourself hanging out with staff at some point. Also, if you are someone who likes to have a drink, you are probably going to have a cocktail with them as well. And even though I am going to tell you why drinking with your staff is a bad idea, I admit that I have occasionally had a beverage or three with my teams throughout the years.

Some restaurants prohibit fraternization with staff after

hours, and the rule makes sense in theory. It would reduce any perceived favoritism and eliminate the possibility of poor alcohol-related choices that could bleed over into the workspace. The rule is a great idea but it is rarely adhered to in reality.

As a restaurant manager, you naturally feel a kinship with your team. When everyone heads to the pub after work, it is tough to always decline the invitation and go home to watch Netflix. So, if you are going to hang out with your staff occasionally, at least do so intelligently.

NEVER FORGET YOU ARE THE BOSS ... THEY DON'T

You are their boss whether you are in the restaurant or not. Believing otherwise is a huge failing of freshman managers, who think that because they are sharing a beer together, that the manager hat comes off. It doesn't. You could tell everyone that it has or even announce it upon your arrival. It doesn't matter. You are still their boss and are always perceived in that manner first.

To further drive home this point, think of the last time you were out with the team and you were introduced to someone new. Did they mention your position? Probably so.

I have noticed that tendency throughout my career. All of us could be relatively the same age and enjoy the same drinks. But when I am introduced to others in a casual setting, my title is invariably mentioned. I realize that they never lost sight of the fact that I was in a position of influence. I could change their schedules, their sections, and even their employment status.

You are always perceived as the boss, and being the boss outside your venue is really not a good thing for you. It means that anything you do will be scrutinized and gossiped about, no matter if it is warranted or not. Spill your drink, the rumors will be that you were drunk. Talk too long to a certain staff member, gossips will say you were trying to hook up with them.

THE PITFALLS OF FRATERNIZING

Hanging out with your team also has a tendency to be seen as a weakness by others. It tells your own boss that your priorities might be more with being liked versus being effective, regardless of whether or not that is the case. I know more than a few owners who measure whether a manager is on "their side" or "the staff side" because they believe that the manager might not be as impactful if he/she constantly fraternizes with the staff. They are not wrong.

Close associations with staff can cloud judgment and make it difficult to lead successfully. When it comes to making tough calls concerning scheduling, performance, and overall employment, it is hard to be seen as fair when you are thought to be friends with certain members of the team.

IF YOU CHOOSE TO DO IT

If you still opt to have after-work drinks with your team, here are a few suggestions to minimize your risk:

- Choose those events where you feel that it is important for you to be with your team. There are likely many others where you should decline the invitation.

- Never be the first one to arrive or the last to leave.

- Always make your rounds and speak with everyone in attendance.

- Only have two drinks max.

- Pay the entire tab up to that point before leaving, unless it is a company-sponsored event.

You should follow those steps because you are their leader. You will establish a presence, make everyone feel included, and defuse any potential issues around the bill.

You don't want your staff buying you drinks. If you cannot afford to cover the bill, find people outside of work to drink with.

Avoid attending exclusive gatherings, like meeting for a drink with just one or two staff members. Try to limit your appearances to larger staff functions and the following day make sure to acknowledge those who were not present, even though that comes with its own problems, such as when you say, "Hey, Todd, I noticed you didn't make it out last night for hair metal karaoke." You might say, "We would have enjoyed having you there." Unfortunately, Todd was probably not invited, which is where the problems occur in such situations. Better to avoid after-work gatherings with staff.

So, you can see why many restaurants discourage this behavior. If you still opt to engage, understand you are battling additional scrutiny. You likely already receive enough within the four walls of your restaurant. In fact, you are probably battling unnecessary negative perceptions in many different directions. That condition just comes with the territory. But those who do not feel like they are in your inner circle will blame their being left out of extracurricular activities for every bad shift or disciplinary action you give them.

Therefore, the real cost of an after-work beverage could be a very unpleasant trip to human resources for you.

Surprise! Chapter Review:
Five Cautionary Rules to Follow
If You Hang Out with Staff

1. Never showing up to exclusive gatherings. Make sure everyone available is invited. The more staff, the better.

2. Always talk to everyone there. Balance your conversations equally so as not to appear to have favorites.

3. Never get hammered. Have two drinks max.

4. Never have anyone buy your drinks. Instead, you should pay the running tab before you leave.

5. Never make a big production of your exit. Just say your goodbye and leave.

Bottom Line: You are taking a risk every time you fraternize with staff. The safe bet is to find people outside of work with whom to socialize.

CHAPTER 21

DATA VERSUS EMOTION

You focus on enthusiasm, gauging how your staff is feeling and who might not be performing at their best. This ranking is based solely on your gut. When you notice that someone is coming across as less than energetic, you address them by saying, "I feel like your energy is really down lately. We need you to be on your top game." *Surprise!* Your staff continues to display disengagement. What should you do?

As a restaurant manager, you will encounter drama from your staff. I have yet to find a place where there isn't some tension among the teams. Such factors inevitably lead to servers being convinced that hosts are purposefully giving them bad tables or bartenders being accused of withholding gratuities from barbacks. And just about all of that infighting is based on nothing more concrete than "I feel host Amy doesn't like me" or "I think bartender Todd is stealing tips."

Although "I think" and "I feel" might be useful in marriage therapy, it hardly counts as evidence. Surrounded by all this emotion, it is easy to think that acknowledging their behavior is the best way to communicate. But it is not.

THE DATA

Data is vital because the decisions you make might affect someone's ability to pay rent. If a host is truly being vindictive and not equally seating a server, then that host should be removed. Same goes for the bartender withholding tips from the barback. It's stealing, simple as that. But you better be correct before you warn or terminate.

Did you cross-reference in your reservation software the number of times that particular host sat the server as opposed to others over the last few months? Did you review the bartender's sales against the barback tip-out for anomalies? What about a good old-fashioned secret shopper or security surveillance review? If not, then you are left with rumors and assumptions, which are never grounds for dismissal.

What about if you want to coach a staff member on ways to improve. If you wish to let a server know they are underperforming and how to improve, do so with data. Talk about their tip percentages, check averages, online review mentions, turn times, tardiness, etc. Those factors translate into tangible data that can be used to measure performance.

On the other hand, saying "I feel you aren't doing a good job" or "I think you can do better" provides zero context. There are no benchmarks for satisfactory improvement. You are managing from emotion, which will never have the impact you want.

Such adherence to facts should extend to any performance review. Many companies offer feedback to their staff on a semi-regular basis, and the importance of the practice cannot be overstated. Without taking time to discuss the goals and next steps with every staff member in the restaurant, you are sending a message that there is no growth and no plan for development. A lack of consistent progress reports also is likely linked to higher turnover rates. That being said, if reviews are not done correctly, they can also have very negative consequences.

THE QUARTERLY REVIEW

My first exposure to a quarterly review was as a young restaurant manager. My employer used a numbered scale, 1–5, ranked from poor to exceptional. Three was considered "satisfactory." The factors included categories like attitude, floor presence, and appearance. The problem I had with it arose from a fundamental difference of how the employer and I each viewed the rating system and his use of emotion-based feedback. I received mostly satisfactory marks, which from an academic standpoint is a "C."

Like many people, I am programmed for top grades, and if I do not receive them I want to be given clear direction on how to achieve better marks immediately. Instead, I was offered general statements like "I feel you could do more on the floor" or "I think you could work on your attitude." None of my employer's comments provided tangible suggestions for improvement. The emotional statements were vague and off-putting. It was a turning point for me with that company. I left soon after.

It's like being told "I think you need to smile more." Not helpful advice for anyone in the history of ever.

Remember that the important part of coaching behavior is "coach." You are on their team, giving them clear direction and detailed strategies on how to win. I'm not sure that the Bulls would have won so many championships if Phil Jackson's locker room speeches were no more helpful than "I feel you aren't giving your best. I think you guys should try harder." Doesn't really do much. Focus on data and take an active role in your teams' improvement, as all of you are—or should be—focused on a common goal.

Surprise! Chapter Review:
Seven "Motivational" Comments Made
by Bad Managers

1. "I know you can bring your energy up."

2. "I believe you can do even better."

3. "You are one of our best when you apply yourself."

4. "Let's turn that frown upside down today."

5. "I think you could be as good as Todd."

6. "Let's make sure you are on your 'A-Game'"

7. "I feel like you have just started showing us who you are."

Bottom Line: When providing feedback, always stick with measurable facts. You must use data to support your assertions, not your emotions.

CHAPTER 22

RESULTS VERSUS EGO

You know how to fix almost every problem in the restaurant. You have told your staff multiple times how to make improvements, yet they don't seem to care about your solutions. *Surprise!* Your team is unwilling to follow your lead. What should you do?

Picture this: Your busser station looks terrible. There is zero organization. Servers and bussers are depositing cleared items in haste. Dirty plates, forks, glasses, and napkins are finding their way into the same bus tub. Not only does it make for more work for the dishwasher, the jumble also means additional laundry charges for stained linens. The entire area is costly, unsightly, and inefficient. Fortunately, you have a solution.

At the next pre-shift, you distribute detailed instructions on where each item should be placed. There is a bin for flatware, one for plates, a rack for glasses, and a bag for linens. You have labeled everything with P-Touch tape and laminated a map of the layout, which is now mounted in the station. After explaining thoroughly, you make sure no one has any questions. They do not. Everyone understands the plan, and it works perfectly— *for one week.*

Why did your idea fail?

The answer is simple: because it came from you and your ego

alone.

Throwing all the dishes in one pile takes less effort than separating them accordingly. Your servers and bussers are focused on returning to the floor and do not see the value in taking the extra time to sort. You can attempt to stress how much more difficult they are making it for the kitchen or how much money you are losing in ruined napkins, but they have no real investment in embracing your solution, beyond your trying to guilt them into making things better for the dishwasher. Such motivation never lasts too long, though.

MAKE YOUR TEAM PART
OF THE SOLUTION

The best way to get a group to agree to increase their effort is if they are a part of the decision process.

Instead of instructing your staff how to fix the problem, consider the impact if you had asked for their help to solve it. In pre-shift, you could bring up the issue: "Has anyone noticed the pile-up in the busser area?"

Once the situation is acknowledged, then lead into "I am at a loss on the best way to tackle this. Does anyone have suggestions?"

You would continue this line of questioning until the team collectively comes up with their solution, which will likely be the same answer you already had but now they feel connected to the idea. They have "buy-in" and are more invested in its success.

INVITE YOUR TEAM TO
SOLVE THE ISSUE

The following is an example of "Discovery Learning." This technique, founded in the 1960s, is often credited to Jerome Bruner, an American psychologist who made significant contributions in the field of cognitive learning theory and educational psychology.[6] Discovery learning occurs when your team is not provided the answer but rather the input to come up with solutions on their own.

The technique works well in a restaurant environment, particularly when you are attempting to develop procedures for everyone to follow. The challenge is that its execution requires you to not have an ego, which is difficult for many managers to embrace.

You can overcome many challenges as long as you are not concerned about ego. It is as true in your job as it is in life. When you appear to have all the answers, you risk being viewed as a know-it-all. Saying "I don't know" to your team will not make you look incapable. Instead, it translates as "I need help," which is a powerful expression to model. In the same way that you want your staff to ask for assistance, requesting it yourself shows them that it is safe to do the same.

In the example of the busser station, you already had a very good solution but not the buy-in from the staff to properly execute. In order to get the team onboard, you would have to say that you didn't have the answer. This admission opens the door for the staff to contribute.

If you are unable to leave your ego behind, you will not successfully execute discovery learning. You cannot inspire others to invest in conclusions if you are always inserting your ideas or opinions. You will only lecture from a base of knowledge, which will only take you so far.

A LITTLE REVIEW TO KEEP YOUR EGO IN CHECK

Here are a few of the strategies from previous chapters and how your ego could get in the way:

Server hiring fellow servers: When staff members have a say in whom they will work alongside, they are more motivated to help those new hires to succeed. Your serving staff will definitely feel a sense of obligation to Todd if they were a part of the decision to bring him on. If you feel you know better and do not wish to include your team in this manner, you are missing out on a great opportunity to empower (Chapter 6: "*Finding Great Staff*").

Witnesses: When you are providing challenging info to a staff member, you must have someone with you to witness the conversation. Arrogance will convince you that step is not needed and that you know how to handle it. The repercussions of such a decision can be devastating (Chapter 11: "*Witness Protection*").

Online reviews: The goal in delivering effective responses is not to prove your point but to acknowledge the guests' disappointment, no matter how incorrect. For example, this tactic might mean apologizing for something that is completely normal. I jokingly refer to such retorts by using the outlandish example, "I am sorry that your water was so wet." Don't make it about being right. If your self-righteousness flares up, you will not recover these guests (Chapter 16: "*Conquering Online Reviews*").

The above examples require you to set your ego aside for the greater good. You are obviously required to have decisive responses in certain situations. If a guest is angry about a foreign object in their salad, and the server asks for help, you cannot respond with "I'm not sure." Your leadership will always be required at times, and you need to be able to rely on your instincts to provide a solution. The difference is that such issues do not require the buy-in of a group.

Just be willing to appear vulnerable at times. You might be surprised at the number of people who reach out, happy to help. You will definitely appreciate the results provided by that simple act of asking for help.

Surprise! Chapter Review:
Building Staff Loyalty by Reducing Your
Ego in Five Easy Steps

1.   Ask for help, even if you think you know the answer.

2.   Allow others to provide suggestions for solutions.

3. Encourage your team to make more decisions in their workplace.

4. Never lay blame for the failures of your team. Take personal responsibility.

5. Always sidestep every compliment, attributing every success to your staff.

Bottom Line: You will always get more accomplished when you focus on your intended result instead of your ego.

CHAPTER 23

THE BOULDER THEORY

You are guarded in your actions, making sure to map out all possible scenarios for failure before proceeding. Your boss does not share your caution, often making moves based on the possibility of future profit instead of the challenges to current operations. The clash results in decisions you find to be unnecessarily hurried. *Surprise!* You are struggling to work with someone because they are so opposite of you. What should you do?

Picture this: There are two teams and two enormous boulders in the middle of a field, each eight feet tall and much too heavy for a single person to budge. The goal is to be the first team to roll it to the edge of the clearing, avoiding the numerous ditches along the way.

Team Headstrong immediately begins pushing with all their might, not concerned about the problems that may lie ahead, or even if they are going in the right direction.

All the while, Team Guarded does not begin to push. These team members take time calculating the exact trajectory of the boulder, devising the optimal route to avoid ditches and as well as the speed it can be moved without losing control. Once all the foreseeable obstacles are determined, they methodically start moving the object toward its goal.

If Team Headstrong is moving relatively in the right direction from the start, they will win nearly every time. They are not swayed by convention and ignore the naysayers. They are focused on moving the boulder as quickly as possible, feeling almost destined for success and not concerned about possible pitfalls. Team Headstrong embraces speed over contemplation. Their pace might seem erratic, even reckless, to those who do not share their philosophy.

Team Guarded is methodical and careful. Not only do these team members see the obvious obstacles, they research where other challenges might be hiding just below the surface. They move unhurried but very rarely in the wrong direction. Although their pace seems slow to those on the other side, it ensures that the boulder doesn't end up in a ditch. Their cautious planning will greatly minimize the possibility of costly errors. It also guarantees that they will likely arrive last, as long as Team Headstrong doesn't make any catastrophic errors.

TEAM HEADSTRONG

In the restaurant world, most owners are on Team Headstrong. They are bold, self-convinced, and willing to take risks in order to win. Their decisions are normally based on potential revenue over the possible impact on current operations.

For example, if an owner feels that they will be able to potentially make more money by extending the restaurant's late-night hours, they will push to make this adjustment immediately. There is likely no "waiting period" to make sure all staff are informed, trained, and prepared. The answer is "now."

Team Headstrong is not careless as much as they are confident and exude a sense of extreme urgency. Of course, their plan could fail spectacularly, and a few of their rapid decisions could even hurt the restaurant, but Team Headstrong lives by hockey legend Wayne Gretzky's famous line: "You miss 100 percent of the shots you don't take."

TEAM GUARDED

Restaurant managers are usually on Team Guarded. They are cautious of pushing limits, concerned about negatively affecting the guest experience or the staff's level of buy-in.

A common example is found with reservations. Many managers will limit the number of available tables online, in case there are substantial walk-ins. Whereas Team Headstrong would take every table and deal with the consequences if they are flooded, Team Guarded knows all too well that the wing-it approach can make for a very negative experience. Even with the best managers, it is difficult to salvage guests who waited 45 minutes for a table because the restaurant was overbooked, no matter how many free drinks you buy them at the bar.

Team Guarded finds value in prudence and errs on the side of safety. They are risk-adverse. By being cautious, they are afforded the best opportunity to create truly exceptional guest visits and provide a measured work environment for their team. They rarely have to dig the boulders out of a ditch because they plotted all possible detours ahead of time.

I am Team Guarded. I consider all the angles. My job is to tell you the risks. I am an odds maker, like a bookie. I can provide data and analytics. But what makes me a great manager—anticipating every possible error—is the same behavior that would prevent me from being an adventurous restaurant owner.

BEING NIMBLE

A major component in any successful business is how willing its leaders are to change. Often, the larger the restaurant group, the less nimble they are. Whereas they might have taken chances when they had only a few locations, caution tends to set in as they grow bigger.

Take the example of modifying a menu item: I worked for a corporate chain where we noticed that the big tomato slice on a new burger was being frequently discarded by the guests.

Through targeted table touches, we determined the thickness was off-putting and made the recommendation to swap the larger single slice with two thinner ones. As it was a large restaurant group, such decisions could not be made at store level. Our finding was submitted to a corporate culinary team, who weighed the merits of the adjustment and taste-tested with other location managers to get their feedback. I remember it taking more than a month before the response came back and the tomato slices were modified. This company was definitely Team Guarded, opting to move the boulder slowly and methodically. The new tomato spec was indeed better received. The downside was that for several weeks, guests still experienced an inferior version while it was being thoroughly investigated.

In contrast, I have also worked with Chef Fabio Viviani. He makes menu changes quite frequently, with the expectation of immediate action. A typical example would be adding a new dish to the menu. The addition could be communicated as late as 4:00 p.m. with the directive for it to be ready for dinner service by 5:00 p.m. This adjustment required that, in the span of one hour, we would:

- Cost the dish and price accordingly.
- Work with kitchen on execution.
- Add to POS and route to correct printers.
- Reprint and stuff menus.
- Train servers and bartenders on ingredients, allergy, and taste.
- Photograph the dish to promote on social media.
- Update the menu on the website and all delivery platforms.

The first time I encountered this, I honestly didn't think it was possible. I was tempted to dig my heels in and explain to Fabio that this entire process would take time to complete. I wanted to roll it out methodically at my pace. Thank goodness I didn't protest or else I wouldn't have learned that it was more achievable than I imagined. Because it was added so rapidly, our guests had the benefit of a great new dish immediately.

EMBRACING YOUR OPPOSITE

You need to balance your restaurant with equal parts Headstrong and Guarded. One is comprised of visionaries who see potential where others might not; the other consists of operators who make sure that all the necessary tools are in place to succeed. With too many headstrong people, you will occasionally go far off course; too many guarded members and you won't move at all.

The challenge is how to work with people who see the world so differently. The key is to first acknowledge that your restaurant isn't a race between two competing teams. It is everyone working toward the common goal of a profitable business. Headstrong people are not the enemy of the Guarded or vice versa. They only have different strategies for success, which both teams should appreciate.

Allow yourself to be open to embracing some of the philosophy from the opposite side. The more I surround myself with Headstrong people, the more I become risk-tolerant and willing to take a few operational chances. The same happens on the flip side, with Guarded people teaching Headstrong to consider a second look before charging forward. In carpentry, this maxim is known as "measure twice, cut once."

Not all owners are Headstrong, and not all managers are Guarded. And much like a growing company, you can start out on one side and later become more on the other. There are no hard-fast rules. You just need to acknowledge which side you are more drawn to and learn to surround yourself with the opposite.

Surprise! Chapter Review:
How to Work with Headstrong People

- Always keep in mind that nearly any action is preferable to inaction.

- Acknowledge that the Headstrong sense of urgency is a truly powerful and useful gift.

- Never challenge their strategies unless you are confident you can provide a better one within the same time frame for execution.

- Remember that great reward requires a level of risk you might be unwilling to take. This challenge, however, does not make it wrong.

Surprise! Chapter Review:
How to Work with Guarded People

- Know that their caution comes from caring about both your success and the company's.

- Acknowledge that they might see challenges ahead that you haven't considered.

- Never openly dismiss cautious advice. Doing so makes you appear arrogant and will demotivate Team Guarded from continuing to watch out for dangers ahead.

- Never forget that the concerns of Guarded team members might be well-founded. If they tell you something is a terrible idea, they could have a point.

Bottom Line: Counterbalances are essential for all team efforts. You must surround yourself with opposite energies, priorities, and strategies for achieving common goals.

CHAPTER 24

SELF-PROMOTION IS SELF-PRESERVATION

You have been working for years as a manager at your restaurant. The owner does not micromanage, and you are left to handle the daily operations. You want to move up in the company. *Surprise!* Other managers are continually being promoted instead of you. What should you do?

If you are running a restaurant, chances are you have bosses, or perhaps owners, to whom you report. You might feel your efforts are being noticed by them on a fairly regular basis. News flash: you're mistaken.

Many bosses function under the "no news is good news" philosophy. If they do not hear anything, they presume everything must be fine. They assume your performance is satisfactory, providing them the opportunity to focus on other aspects of the business. That attitude is not an indictment of ownership. They have a myriad of necessary responsibilities to address beyond rating your daily productivity.

It is easy to see a no-boast posture as job security in that you are not on their radar. Unfortunately, that perception likely means that the only time your boss addresses your performance is when there has been an error. That view leads to your work being judged on the least number of screw-ups, simply because your successes are not being tallied.

The downside of being overlooked is why self-promotion is so essential. If your boss is often reminded of your successes, then failings can be judged in perspective. Self-promotion provides a counterbalance to any negativity.

Simply put, you are applying for your job every single day, both the one you have and the one that you want. Self-promotion helps to justify your current existence and increases your chances for advancement. No one else will sing your praises the way you can.

DON'T LISTEN TO MOM

You were taught as a child to be humble, never wanting to appear boastful or arrogant. I often encounter talented managers who are waiting for advancement but are unwilling to highlight their achievements to their bosses. The moment you abandon the mentality that others will recognize your efforts automatically, the sooner you will advance your career.

You cannot allow modesty to keep you from self-celebrating. I am not suggesting a social media campaign about your genius or showing up to work wearing an "I Rule" t-shirt—nothing that obvious. Your communication needs to be professional, spotlighting achievements, and providing ideas to fix business deficits.

The following are three tactics guaranteed to keep your name at the top of the promotions list:

Status Reports: Usually provided as an email, this account is a periodic snapshot of the status of the restaurant in relation to established goals, including strategies to improve sales performance, labor percentages, and F&B COGS. It should track progress over the previous week and the prior year.

If a status update structure is not currently in use, or lacks all pertinent information, you have an excellent opportunity to be the architect of new correspondence. Make sure to include every possible department on such emails (owners, managers, events, marketing, culinary, accounting, etc.). This method ensures that the full team is joining the conversation and focused on a common goal. The report is also a weekly reminder that you are actively monitoring the profitability of the company.

Initiatives: This item is a key component in self-promotion because it is a great chance to offer new strategies. In the same manner that you communicate the status update, you should submit your ideas to the entire group. The fact that you continue to flood in-boxes with your worthy suggestions—for improving sales, decreasing labor, managing overhead expenses, and controlling COGS—keeps you on the mind of those who have influence over your future.

Include as many people as possible about your ideas. Just never omit your direct report. It is one thing to have a conversation that includes multiple leaders, but it is a far different thing for you to leapfrog in an attempt to curry favor. Doing so will only earn you mistrust from your superior and the label of sycophant with the owner.

Also, don't get discouraged if your recommendations are not implemented or even if no one responds at all. Keep in mind, this action is a concerted effort on your part to show that you have an entrepreneurial mind. Depending on the size of your restaurant group, you might be one of dozens or even hundreds of restaurant managers in the organization. Deluging in-boxes on a near daily basis sets you apart. It shows that you are developing solutions, not just maintaining the status quo.

Most importantly, once you begin your campaign of self-promotion, you cannot stop. Nothing is more detrimental than getting on your employers' radar with great ideas, only to have them notice that you abandon your communication soon after.

Requesting Responsibility: The third key to advancement is to act as though you have already received the promotion. You are far more likely to be rewarded for what you have accomplished instead of a promise of what you will do once given the job. You must have your hand up for any task, requesting more responsibility at every turn. You should be on the lookout for opportunities that others do not wish to perform, or better yet, that currently aren't even on the radar. These areas are valuable focuses that others simply have not tackled yet.

You can often find opportunities in managing overhead expenses. Here are just a few that I find that are commonly under-examined in restaurants and ways to improve them:

- **Scheduling Waste Retrieval**: Make a daily log of the amount of garbage in the dumpsters and determine the necessary number of pickups each week. You likely will uncover that less trash is deposited on certain days, allowing you to reduce the frequency of collection.

- **Examining Linen Pars**: Many companies charge based on your predetermined inventory pars, not usage. For example, if you have 2,000 cloth napkins as your par, but only use 1,400 in a week, you are still charged for 2,000. Pull usage reports bimonthly and adjust accordingly.

- **Credit Card Processing**: Costs for processing fluctuate, requiring periodic bids from other vendors to make sure you are receiving the best rates. Examine and reassess every 90 days.

Fewer garbage collections, accurate linen pars, and lowered processing rates will show measurable differences to the bottom line. Decreasing overhead expenses offers so many ways to improve profit. As you spearhead various efforts, you will display your ability to think beyond the traditional avenues, and the more you achieve, the more material you have for self-promotion.

Now that you provide status reports, pitch new initiatives, and are always willing to tackle the difficult tasks, your efforts should equate to a promotion. That said, you still might have to lobby for it. Ask for a performance review, typically on the anniversary of your initial hire date. Have a salary adjustment amount ready, and be confident in your worth. Don't pick a higher number and assume you will be negotiating. You're not buying a car.

Fortunately, if you have been highlighting your achievements throughout the year, you won't have to justify why you deserve your raise. They will already know.

Surprise! Chapter Review:
Five Steps to Becoming Your Own PR Agent

On a regular basis, email the following information to all departments:

1. Frequent status reports on sales, labor, and overhead expenses. Write it up so that they know you are focusing on constantly improving the restaurant's operations.

2. Strategies to build sales and decrease labor. It doesn't matter if every idea doesn't work, only that you were the one coming up with them.

3. Your willingness to take on as many responsibilities as possible. Make sure the owners know you already "have your hand up" to tackle any task.

4. Your desire to oversee the most challenging and least beloved jobs.

5. Your focus on the overlooked aspects that you are more than happy to address.

Bottom Line: If you don't establish clear, consistent communication with decision makers about your achievements, you are choosing to be passive in your career growth.

CHAPTER 25

DOING THE MATH

Tasked with making your restaurant profitable, you are struggling with how much to charge on your menu. What is the standard, and what formulas are needed to arrive at those numbers? When you became a restaurant manager, you never thought that it would involve so much math. *Surprise!* Proper calculations are an enormous requirement in order to be successful. What should you do?

There are three main components to consider when talking about managing the bottom line—labor, COGS, and overhead expenses. Whatever is left over is basically profit. This elementary view is admittedly an oversimplification, but in terms of what you can control, it is a good starting point.

LOGICAL LABOR

Labor includes all hourly staff and salary managers, plus all applicable payroll taxes and benefits. Although the calculation does vary based on concept, a typical maximum allowable is 30 percent. This amount roughly breaks down to 8 percent for FOH staff, 13 percent for BOH, and 9 percent for salaries. Again, not an exact science, but you know that your servers, bartenders, and support staff are paid tipped minimum wage, which accounts for why your FOH labor numbers are nearly half of the BOH labor impact. As an example, let's examine a $3M restaurant. At these sales, 9 percent for salary equals $270,000 to split among managers and chefs.

Labor is the most controllable expense in your restaurant. When you make your staff schedules, use sales from previous week as a guide, measured against your maximum percentages. Using the numbers from above, weekly sales rounded to $60,000 you have:

- 8 percent for FOH staff = $4,800 allowable

- 13 percent for BOH staff = $7,800 allowable

- 9 percent for salary = $5,400 allowable

The challenge comes when you experience a decrease in sales and how it affects what you can spend on staff in relation to management. Salaries obviously don't fluctuate. They are a fixed cost. Using the figure above, if you are spending $270,000 in salary, that $5,192 actual per week will have to come out either way. So, if your sales were $48,000 (not $60,000), then it gets much harder to stay within budget.

- $5,192 for salary @ $48,000 = $42,808 left = 10.82 percent for salary

- If your max labor is 30 percent, then you only have 19.18 percent instead of 21 percent for staffing = $9,206

With weekly sales at $48,000, you have a 27-percent decrease. It is imperative that you schedule accordingly. Stagger the in-times for your team based on estimated volume, and make sure to make cuts to the floor and kitchen once the rush begins to subside. Also, examine your higher-wage positions and see if management can alleviate their labor impact. If you can help cover the front door, that duty will eliminate one host shift for the night—and probably your largest FOH hourly wage.

COGS: THEORETICAL

Next is COGS, which is the amount required to actually obtain or create the item you are selling. If a can of beer costs the restaurant $1.50 to bring in, and you sell it for $6, your COGS is 25 percent. The following are standard COGS thresholds:

- Food > 30 percent
- Beer > 22 percent
- Wine > 25 percent
- Liquor > 18 percent

Again, those calculations also vary greatly by concept and location. Quick service restaurants will likely have much lower food COGS than in fine-dining establishments. Also, the market will probably allow you to charge more for alcohol in affluent areas of major cities than you can competitively price in suburban areas.

Using the above percentages with a sales ratio of 60 percent food, 20 percent liquor, 10 percent beer, and 10 percent wine, you can determine your target overall COGS. Let's say you have $1M in sales. The calculation would be the following:

- Food: 60 percent in sales = $600,000. At 30 percent COGS = $180,000 spent.

- Beer: 10 percent in sales = $100,000. At 22 percent COGS = $22,000 spent.

- Wine: 10 percent in sales = $100,000. At 25 percent COGS = $25,000 spent.

- Liquor: 20 percent in sales = $200,000. At 18 percent COGS = $36,000 spent.

- Total sales = $1,000,000. Total spent = $263,000. Overall COGS = 26.3 percent.

You should periodically run a product mix (p-mix) of your sales to determine your true ratios and to determine when they fluctuate. In the above example, if your overall target is 26.3 percent, but you are trending to more than 60 percent in food sales, you know that you will have to adjust either your prices or your expectations.

WHAT TO CHARGE ON YOUR MENU

Determining the cost of an item is imperative before adding it to the menu. COGS is calculated in a simple equation: **Take how much an item costs to make and divide it by the menu price.** For example, let's examine a grilled chicken sandwich and a possible breakdown:

- Chicken breast = $1.50
- Sourdough roll = $0.30
- Lettuce leaf = $0.03
- Tomato slice = $0.06
- Onion slice = $0.04
- Pickle spear = $0.08
- Garlic aioli = $0.07
- Total = $2.08 COGS

If you sell the sandwich for $7.49, then you would divide it into $2.08, thus making it a 27.77 percent COGS. For every dollar you make on the sandwich, $0.28 goes to paying for the raw materials. Of course, you can adjust your COGS by raising your price or lowering the cost (and often the quality) of the materials but your audience might not like the end result.

Whereas food cost estimating can be challenging at times, beverage is a bit simpler to measure, as it comes in a uniform standard (750-ml liquor bottles, 15.5-gal kegs, etc.).

Kegs: A 15.5-gallon keg (1,984 oz) holds 124 pints (16 oz). Assuming four pints are wasted for pour-offs (initial foam, head), the remainder is 120 pints per keg. If a keg costs $180, then each beer would be $1.50. If you sold that beer for $6, then your COGS would be 25 percent. But if your target COGS is 22 percent, then you must charge at least $6.82 (**Formula = cost/ percentage = 1.50/0.22**).

Bottled Beer: Divide the cost by the number in the case. If a case of 24 costs $32, then each bottle would be $1.33. If you sell it for $6, your COGS is 22.16 percent.

Liquor: A 750-ml bottle of liquor holds 25.4 ounces. Traditional pours are 1.5 ounces. Assuming that 1.4 ounces are lost in waste, there are 16 single drinks per bottle. If a vodka bottle costs $24, then 1.5 ounces would be $1.50. If you sell a vodka for $8.50, then your COGS is 17.65 percent.

Wine: A 750-ml bottle of wine holds 25.4 ounces. Assuming that 1.4 ounces are lost in waste and that the wine is served in six-ounce portions, there are four glasses in a bottle. If possible, you want one glass to pay for the bottle. If it cost $9, then charge $9 a glass, making your COGS 25 percent. As wine turns quickly, the waste potential is high. Keep close tabs on the quantity on hand.

COGS: ACTUAL

Up to this point, we have discussed what the costs *should* be, the theoretical percentages based on straightforward calculations. But in order to determine what your COGS *actually* is, you must take a detailed, accurate inventory. Although some concepts say to perform this monthly, weekly counts will give you the ability to react quicker if you see that your numbers are inflated.

Whether you use an inventory software platform or simply an Excel file, you will need to assign value to each inventory item. As you receive invoices for your order, you must compare those amounts to your numbers to make sure there has not been a fluctuation.

Once you take inventory, you will have a total amount on hand for every department. The major groups are liquor, bottle beer, draft beer, wine, food, nonalcoholic beverage, and possibly retail, although you can split these into subcategories if you wish. For example, you can split liquor into vodka, gin, bourbon, etc., or food into produce, meat, dry goods, etc. Subcategories will allow you to dig deeper when anomalies arise.

Once you have the amounts assigned to your categories, you will need to determine the usage—that is, what product you actually sold between your current inventory and the last one. The formula for usage is: **beginning inventory + invoices – ending inventory**.

Once you have your usage, then divide it by your sales to get your actual COGS. For example, you might start the beginning of the period with $7,000 in food inventory and have $6,000 at the end. During that time, if you sold $28,000 in food and paid $6,500 in food invoices, the formula would be:

- $7,000 (beginning inventory) plus $6,500 (invoices) minus $6,000 (end inventory) = $7,500 usage

- $7,500 (total usage) divided by $28,000 (food) = 0.267 = 26.7-percent food costs

MANAGING COGS EFFECTIVELY

Think of your theoretical as your target numbers but use your actual as your real data. The difference in the two has much to do with how your COGS is managed. Just behind labor, COGS is your most controllable expense. When you see that your actual COGS is climbing beyond your target numbers, you will need to investigate four key factors: waste, theft, portioning, and calculation.

Waste: If your kitchen is prepping too many burgers and the meat goes bad, it will throw your costs off. This effect is the same when bartenders toss a mistake cocktail. Waste logs and comp tabs are necessary to track these occurrences, and you should review for trends and work with your team to minimize errors.

Theft: If you know that someone is taking steak and whiskey out the back door, that situation is obviously an issue. But theft is often not so blatant. Examples include when bartenders give out free drinks or managers order food without ringing it into the POS. To account for such practices is why you have a comp button so everything can be tracked for inventory.

Portioning: If the portion for fries calls for six ounces but the line cook is serving seven, then he is losing you money. The biggest culprit in this overage is the cook's not measuring with a scale or measured scoop. Cooks using their hands for measurement can throw COGS off tremendously. This discrepancy is akin to not using jiggers behind the bar. If untrained bartenders eyeball it instead of measuring, they will pour your profit on that drink down the drain. Do the math. If shots increase to 2 ounces, then that $24 bottle of vodka goes from being 18.75-percent COGS to 25 percent. Significant!

Calculation Error: This area is in reference to faulty math in the COGS calculation, often due to an increased expense not taken into consideration. If the price of avocados goes up 20 percent, you will need to reexamine what you are charging for guacamole. Recalculate all COGS every month, using the most recent pricing reflected on your invoices.

CONTROLLING MORE THAN YOU THINK

The third component in managing your bottom line is the category of overhead expenses. Let's make a distinction. Fixed costs are those that we cannot alter. Rent is a prime example. There is nothing you can usually do to lower that cost. But there are a lot more controllable expenses that you can make sure are not unnecessarily inflated.

For example, you might think your payments for worker's compensation is a fixed cost but you can indirectly affect what you owe. The monthly payment is based on what you remit in wages. If you are spiking labor, your bill will be higher. More substantially, worker's compensation will go up if you have a claim, so make sure you provide a clean, safe environment (dry floors, proper kitchen mats, safety-focused staff).

That variation is true for most bills. If you leave the air conditioning on when you are closed, your energy bill will climb. If someone else is dumping their garbage in your bins, your waste-removal costs rise. Reviewing your monthly statements is key, especially comparing it to prior months. If you witness an increase, you need to investigate.

The most controllable of these costs come from the goods that you purchase and the vendors you use. Make sure you are not unnecessarily using expensive to-go containers, review your linen statement to see if you need to adjust your napkin pars, monitor all invoices to see if you are now being billed more for the same product, and watch for delivery fees and service charges that were not previously agreed upon. You should build relationships with your vendors and sit down with them periodically to see if options are available for better pricing.

It is harder to put a target goal for all overhead expenses, but for the sake of this discussion, I will select 30 percent, including rent. Now apply this amount to the 30-percent max for labor and the 27-percent max for COGS to equal 87 percent, which brings 13 percent down to the bottom line. That number is before ownership distribution and investor payment.

If you are able to keep your labor in check, COGS low, and overhead expenses in line, then you are in a great position to have a profitable restaurant. Learn to master the financial aspects and you will have a very bright future in this industry.

Surprise! Chapter Review:
Top 10 Steps to Help Improve Your Bottom Line

1. Use sales data from previous weeks to determine staffing needs by department.

2. Monitor volume nightly and cut back staff at appropriate times according to volume.

3. If you can cover an hourly responsibility with a salaried manager, do so.

4. Schedule meetings with your linen vendors and waste-removal providers to see if you might be able to adjust the frequency of your service or negotiate a better price.

5. Take inventory weekly to monitor whether actual COGS in any department is out of line.

6. Take inventory nightly for any possible high-theft items, including kitchen proteins and ultra-premium liquors.

7. Monitor bartenders during service for overpouring or for drinks not rung into the POS.

8. Update your theoretical COGS for all menu items monthly, based on your most recent invoices and p-mix.

9. Monitor portion sizes of food items and address with chef as needed.

10. Educate your staff on the four factors that affect COGS and how they can help be part of the solution.

Bottom Line: Properly managing labor, COGS, and overhead expenses is the key to a profitable restaurant.

CHAPTER 26

DID YOU LEARN ANYTHING?

Now that we have discussed your reasons for being in the restaurant industry and ways to improve proficiency and reduce stress levels, *Surprise!...* it is time for a quiz.

The following situations address 10 common restaurant scenarios. If you have finished reading the book and are taking this test, you will have a leg-up. If you flipped to this first, you might want to go back a few chapters, especially if you fail. Best of luck.

1. Todd is upset. He is rarely given the section by the window—the moneymaker spot. Furthermore, he remarks that Amy is frequently stationed there. Todd is correct in his assessment. Although he is a competent server, Amy is truly exceptional, often receiving compliments and guest requests. How do you handle Todd's concerns?

   a. Explain to Todd that the sections are evenly distributed and that he should focus more on his work, not the assignments of others.

   b. Swap out Amy and give Todd the opportunity to work the moneymaker spot to see if he might improve.

c. Tell Todd he simply isn't as good as Amy, detailing specific reasons.

d. Tell Todd if he does not like his section, he doesn't have to work at your restaurant.

Answer (a) is a cop-out, addressing the issue by basically lying. The assignments aren't even, as you are placing the top servers in your best sections based on a logical business decision.

Answer (d) is basically threatening termination. As mentioned in Chapter 9 (*"How to Lose Good People"*), this response is something you must never do. You should appreciate your staff's willingness to work for you, not the other way around.

Many might select (b) because they feel it is supportive for Todd. He is given the opportunity to work the windows and the manager can assess his progress. Sounds like a win, correct? Wrong. Placing him there will not only demotivate Amy but will not give Todd any tools to succeed. He will ultimately fail and then you are saddled with a much harder conversation—one that will likely lead to Todd leaving and Amy feeling unfairly penalized.

The answer is (c). Have an honest conversation with Todd, and tell him he is not on the same level as Amy, using data to support your assertion. Rather than stating "Amy has a great personality" or "Guests really like her," talk about measurables: Amy has higher tip percentages, quicker turn times, better check averages, frequent Yelp mentions, and more requests from returning guests. Once you have explained your reasons, you now owe it to Todd to teach him how to improve. Run mock service trials, observe him with guests, determine why he is not at the same level, and then work to get him there. After this effort, if he isn't capable of commanding the best sections, then be honest with yourself and with Todd. Review Chapter 18 ("*Embracing Blunt Criticism*") for more.

2. A new bourbon, Cornadrinkia, is on the market. Despite its terrible name, you agree to add it to your whiskey list. Packaged in a 750-ml bottle, your cost is $38.82. Your restaurant pours all bourbons at two ounces, served over a custom logo two-inch ice cube, which runs $1.05 each. According to budget, all whiskeys must have a 19-percent COGS. How much do you have to sell one Cornadrinkia for?

   a. $14.50

   b. $16.10

   c. $21.63

   d. $25.36

   First, convert 750 ml to ounces (25.36 oz), and then divide that number by the price ($38.82), which equals $1.53/oz. The drink is two ounces ($3.06) plus the fancy ice cube ($1.05) equals $4.11, the actual cost to create it. Now you must factor in the 19-percent COGS by taking $4.11 and dividing by 0.19. The answer is (c).

   By the way, if the same drink did not have the fancy ice, you would be able to charge $5.53 less ($16.10) and still maintain the 19-percent COGS goals. This calculation is always something to consider when adding garnishes to cocktails. Review Chapter 25 ("*Doing the Math*") for more.

3. There are guests in the dining room cursing loudly. Their behavior has begun to ruin the experience for others, with one table asking to move and another hastily getting their check and leaving. Upon requesting discretion from the unruly patrons, they inform you they are investors in your restaurant and will contin-

ue to conduct themselves as they wish. A quick call to the owner confirms their identities. You are also strictly instructed not to approach them again. Five minutes later, a member of your staff comes to you upset. One of the investors addressed the server with an offensive slur. What do you do?

a. Ask the server how they wish to handle the situation.

b. Throw out the investor immediately.

c. Approach the table and ask whether or not the comment was made.

d. Unsure. The answer depends on what the slur was.

There are so many wrong options here and only one correct answer.

(a) Asking the server for an opinion is weak and puts the burden on the person who received the slur. This choice is a poor tactic that some managers use to see if the server is willing to just let it go, which they are hoping is the case. But the investor's behavior is a clear sign of harassment, and it is a manager's responsibility to determine how to proceed.

(c) Approaching the table to ask is futile because they will simply deny it, which will leave you slinking away with the issue unresolved. It also sends the message to your staff that you do not believe them. It is unlikely that someone would make up having a table hurl slurs at them. Not impossible but not likely.

(d) Judging based on the severity of the slur is ludicrous. The last thing you should do is attempt to minimize the impact of a hateful comment based on your interpretation, instead of the one who received it.

The correct answer is (b): Eject immediately from the building. You should take this action with any guest who is physically or verbally abusive to your team, no matter who they are. If your owner is upset, it's a worthy battle to pick. Also, you will likely need to pull from petty cash to make sure the server does not lose compensation for speaking out against unacceptable behavior.

If you do not have the backs of your staff, they will never trust or respect you. Review Chapter 9 (*"How to Lose Good People"*) for more.

4. You find that your new bar supervisor, who reports to you, is hanging out with several members of the staff after hours. Although your company does not explicitly forbid this behavior, it nevertheless has prompted feelings of alienation among those who are not regularly invited. You have already addressed your concerns with this supervisor previously, who assured you it would end. But you recently discovered that this activity hasn't stopped. How do you handle?

   a. Ignore, as it isn't taking place during work and not necessarily in conflict with restaurant policy.

   b. Occasionally hang out with the bar supervisor and the selected staff to make sure nothing more inappropriate is happening.

   c. Write up the bar supervisor for their lack of professional judgment.

   d. Plan to replace the bar supervisor.

Although you cannot do (a) and ignore the behavior as it is affecting the workplace, (b) socializing so you can chaperone won't solve the problem either. And (c) write-ups rarely have a lasting, or even positive effect, not to mention you cannot document something that isn't necessarily against the rules.

The challenge is that you asked the bar supervisor to stop doing something and they agreed that they would.

At this point, it doesn't really matter what the request was. It could be something as dumb as "please stop wearing green." When asked, they had two choices: agree to comply or opt to decline.

Instead he/she agreed to stop and then made no attempt to do so. Unfortunately, this outcome points to a person who will tell you what you want to hear and then continue to wear green. This individual is not leadership material. The answer is (d): plan to remove.

The supervisor made a choice that is likely affecting their ability to lead. It has already prompted certain team members to feel alienated. He/she made a risky decision and it is backfiring in your restaurant. You were right to request this behavior to cease. Review Chapter 20 ("*The Real Cost of an After-Work Drink*") for more.

5. You are in the midst of hiring hosts. Which of the following interview questions is safe to ask?

    a. "Are you married?"

    b. "Are you fluent in any languages besides English?"

    c. "Where were you born?"

    d. "What year did you graduate high school?"

Option (a) addresses family status, which is not an acceptable topic for an interview. Employers could discriminate based on whether or not someone is married, perhaps incorrectly believing a single person might have more time to dedicate to the position.

Option (c) addresses nationality. Questions that might address an interviewee's citizenship or country of origin are not allowed. Such a question often happens in interviews when the applicant has a pronounced accent.

Option (d) is basically a work-around to ask someone their age, a definite off-limits conversation. Much like family status and nationality, any inquiry related to age is also another characteristic covered by the Equal Employment Opportunity Commission.

The correct answer is (b), although there is a stipulation. Whereas you cannot ask someone if English is their *first* language (as that can be viewed as country of origin question), you can ask if they are fluent in any languages as long as it applies to their job. Being bilingual helps tremendously in many restaurants, but if it does not apply to yours, you cannot ask. Review Chapter 3 (*"Questions You Cannot Ask"*) for more.

6. Although your food COGS has remained steady at 26 percent for months, this week's statement shows the cost at 30 percent. You have already verified that both the beginning and ending inventories were performed correctly and that all invoices were submitted and recorded accurately. Which of the following could *not* be a viable reason for the recent increase?

   a. The refrigerator fan broke overnight, requiring the disposal of multiple proteins.

   b. A staff member works at a food truck on the weekends and has been taking product—which was already close to expiration—to his other job.

   c. The cost of pork spiked tremendously due to a large portion of the pig population, which have now become inedible zombies.

   d. Instead of ordering three bags of sugar, chef accidently ordered 300, which have filled your dry storage. Your food supplier refuses to allow a return.

   e. The new line cook thought the steak add-on for your top-selling Mediterranean salad was a full 10-ounce filet, instead of the correct four-ounce skirt portion.

Having established that the inventories and invoices were recorded correctly, there are only four factors to examine when COGS go askew: waste, theft, calculation, and portioning.

Option (a) is waste. The food was not held at the proper temperature so it had to be discarded. Other examples include a spilled bag of flour, expired milk, and dropping chicken on the floor (and opting not to use the flawed five-second rule).

Option (b) is theft. If someone is taking meat out the back door, your costs are going to go up. Pretty straightforward. However, stealing is not always so blatant. Obviously, when a bartender gives out shots without charging, it is theft, but so is the unrecorded shift drink after closing. For both waste and theft, the way to track is by ringing it in the POS. Whether it is the remake on the chicken or a shot for some friends, as long as it is tracked and comped, then your COGS will not be negatively affected. Your comps will.

Option (c) is calculation. As discussed in the Question #2 about Cornadrinkia, you arrive at your percentage by dividing cost by price. If pork prices spike due to limited availability so will your numbers.

Option (e) is portioning. If the recipe called for one amount and you are serving significantly more, your food costs will suffer. You see similar increases a lot with liquor costs from overpouring.

The answer that is not a viable reason is (d). As long as you are taking proper inventory and there isn't the possibility of imminent expiration, you can have as much product as you want on your shelves without hurting your costs. Yes, it 100 percent affects your cash flow but not your percentages.

Sugar stays good for two years, so spoilage really isn't a factor. If your inventory has 300 bags at the beginning of the week and 299 at the end, your week's "usage" is only one bag. Usage is what COGS is based on, not your total amount on hand. Review Chapter 25 ("*Doing the Math*") for more.

7. Your restaurant receives an online review, detailing a guest's negative experience with their food, cocktails, and service. They were particularly critical of their server, Amy, who they felt neglected them the entire evening. Amy is one of your best. You remember the table because they sent back their lasagna for being cold and a craft cocktail for not having enough alcohol, both of which you comped. However, the guests never mentioned poor service. What should you do?

   a. Reach out publicly to question why they didn't mention the service issues to you at the time.

   b. Reach out privately to defend Amy's service, citing her consistent compliments from other guests.

   c. Reach out privately to invite them back for a completely free experience for the reviewer plus a friend.

   d. Nothing. You already comped them items while at your restaurant, and their review is a blatant attempt for more free stuff.

This question is a good example of what you *should* do versus what you might *want* to do. You might want to follow option (a) and question their reasoning for not discussing the poor service sooner. However, such an inquiry will immediately be perceived as defensive to both the review's author and anyone else who reads it.

You might want to go for option (b) and privately argue your case for Amy's service. Now, though, you are more focused on being right than acknowledging the guest's obvious disappointment.

You definitely might be tempted to go with option (d). Just do nothing. It can be exhausting to revisit a guest complaint, particularly when you were a part of the initial attempts to improve their experience. By allowing yourself to dismiss the review as an attempt to get more free stuff, you are "playing detective." Soon, you will find more reasons why you shouldn't answer even more reviews, overlooking genuine disappointment and driving your ratings down.

The answer is (c). You have to assume that this is someone who truly had a miserable experience in your restaurant. Their drinks were weak, and their food was cold. Maybe they didn't mention the service because Amy was still visible during your table touches, or perhaps they just wanted to get done with their meal and leave as quickly as possible.

Either way, they left disappointed, which means you did not do a proper recovery. Inviting them back for a comp visit is the only way to change their opinion of your restaurant and, hopefully, the star rating. Review Chapter 16 (*"Conquering Online Reviews"*) for more.

8. Your POS system goes out in the middle of service. Although it is working properly now, the temporary outage affected ticket times for both the bar and the kitchen. Your staff are furiously hustling to get drinks and food out as quickly as possible. What is the best course of action you should take?

    a. Jump behind the bar and start making drinks.

    b. Plant yourself at the front door and have the host who handles reservations move to seating guests.

    c. Talk to tables to gauge their level of satisfaction or frustration, even if you have already spoken to them previously.

    d. Call the POS company to make sure another outage doesn't happen.

Option (a) will likely cause more chaos than assistance. Your presence behind the bar, especially if you are not incredibly well-versed and proficient at making drinks, will only make your bartenders uneasy and interrupt their flow.

Option (b) removes someone entirely from their established skill, running the reservations, and having them walk guests to tables. Not only does this action replace a team member who has more practice than you do at the host stand, both Options (a) and (b) lock you to a specific spot. You cannot help the full restaurant if you are only in one location. It would be far better if you were the one to help seat, and you could observe other aspects of the dining room and address concerns as needed.

Option (d) is probably necessary but not in the moment. If your POS is unstable, then this flakiness definitely needs to be addressed with tech support. That being said, you can make this call a bit later. Your immediate concern should be the long ticket times and the effect on your guests.

All the aforementioned reveals why option (c) is the correct answer. Your best move is to make sure the delays are not destroying your guests' experience. Touch tables multiple times and inquire about their evening and their speed of service. If there is a plate to clear or a drink to refill, you can use this opportunity for additional reasons to engage with the guests. If you encounter frustration at a table, you are present and ready to make their visit better.

During a rush, particularly due to an unforeseen technical problem, it is easy to want to roll your sleeves up and pitch in. Often, the best course of action is to model a calm demeanor to your team, interact frequently with your guests, and provide assistance that does not get in the way of the staff. Review Chapter 10 (*"Sleeves Up or Down"*) for more.

9. During a table touch, you encounter an irate guest who claims that they have just contracted food poisoning from eating their medium-well ribeye. You know that the incubation period for most foodborne illness is a minimum of four hours. The guest's steak arrived at the table only five minutes ago. You are very confident that the sudden illness is not food poisoning. How do you respond?

   a. Explain to the guest that foodborne illnesses do not react in this manner and reassure that all your steaks are top quality and safe. Charge full price.

   b. Let the guest know that they will not be charged for their steak, but be careful not to apologize.

   c. Apologize, comp the full meal, and offer to call for medical attention.

   d. Offer to send out a round of desserts for the table.

Answer (a) will only get you into an argument. You cannot educate the guest on why they are wrong. They likely had a stomach bug long before arriving at your restaurant and legitimately feel ill. But to that guest, the poisoning is real, so you should not attempt to dismiss it. You also might be of the opinion it's a scam to get a free meal. It's possible and actually really sad. Review Chapter 17 (*"Taking the Second Step"*). Can you imagine having the type of life that you are forced to defraud restaurants in order to eat?

Some restaurants employ (b) as a way of dealing with food poisoning claims. It is similar to car accidents when you are advised to exchange information, but never say "sorry." The concern is by doing so, you are somehow admitting fault. I am not a fan of this tactic.

When I was much younger, I had a chicken Caesar from a famous restaurant chain. Eight hours later, I ended up in the emergency room on an IV. Classic food poisoning—I was spouting like a two-headed sprinkler, if you need the visual. The next morning, I called the location and said, "I wanted to let you know about the chicken Caesar. I am not looking for anything, just passing along the information so you can investigate on your end." The manager swore it was impossible. I reassured him it was the only thing I had consumed that day. He got even more defensive and angry. I didn't go back to that chain for nearly 20 years, stubbornly because of that sole experience with the manager's handling of my call.

Option (d) not only doesn't address the issue but relies on the common response of free desserts. This person believes your restaurant poisoned them. Offering more food is not the solution.

Option (c) is the best answer. Apologize that they are feeling ill. Ask if they need an ambulance. If they refuse, ask multiple times. Privately list in your incident report the number of times you asked. Documenting your attempts to get them help will show that you took their claim seriously.

Comp their entire meal. You must function from the belief that this person is physically ill and that they think your food was the cause. Your apology should address how they feel ("I'm so sorry that you are feeling sick") but not confirming any poisoning. In this case, you shouldn't agree with their claim that it's food poisoning but you cannot disagree openly either. Although you know their self-diagnosis is wrong, you should never defend when faced with a complaint.

Had the manager from my experience just apologized on the phone ("Sorry that happened") and asked how I was feeling, I wouldn't have held a grudge. I still won't order the chicken Caesar there again.

Recovering a guest experience is not about being right. Review Chapter 15 (*"How to Fix a Broken Table"*) for more.

10. After multiple documented verbal and written warnings, you fire a server for excessive tardiness. A witness was present during the termination and you followed all policies correctly. A few days later, a staff member approaches you at work and shows a Facebook post on their phone. You are being spoken about online personally by the former server who has called you an a-hole and is encouraging people to stop frequenting your restaurant. It has garnered attention among your team, with both current and former staff members either supporting you or agreeing with the post. How do you deal with this situation?

    a. You don't. You simply pretend it does not exist.

    b. Address individually with those current staff members who responded negatively, reassuring them that you are not an a-hole.

    c. Craft a thoughtful, well-written response to post on Facebook, defending yourself.

    d. Reach out to the former server, plead your case, and ask to have the post removed.

This one is very tough not to react emotionally or to see the post as anything but vindictive. But much like a negative Yelp, the author is very disappointed and feels this action is their best platform to air their grievances. Although tempting, if you write a response on Facebook (c), it will only show that you are now a part of the conversation. Now the former team member is emboldened and knows you are paying attention to their posts. Such interaction will likely result in additional negative comments. Also, much like publicly rather than privately answering a review, you will never be able to have a constructive dialogue in a public forum.

Now, we are at option (d). If your intention is to have the post removed, don't bother reaching out. Not only are you showing that their tactics are having an effect on you but you are making it about the post and not the reasons behind it. I have attempted this one unsuccessfully several times. On behalf of a manager who was being maligned, I once asked a former bartender to remove his negative post. He agreed on the phone, then updated his message to say my restaurant begged him to remove it. My attempt just poured kerosene on the flames. The bartender posted because he felt powerless, and my request provided the leverage he wanted.

Option (b) would make for a very uncomfortable and inappropriate workplace. Your staff made comments about you in a public forum, which is their absolute right. You cannot celebrate your supporters any more than you should plead your case with your detractors. It is an online conversation, away from your restaurant.

Option (a) is the correct answer. Although you want to "clear your name," you are battling perception. The more you publicly address the accusations, the more attention you are bringing to the conversation about your being an a-hole. If one of your bartenders states online that you are a Martian, it shouldn't bother you. You absolutely know you aren't from Mars, so the accusations are silly and don't warrant a response. Review Chapter 13 (*"The Art of Termination"*) for more.

Finally, the reason you are so upset is perhaps you think that the comment has some validity. What bothers you the most when faced with criticism usually is subconsciously your greatest concern. The next time you find yourself becoming defensive to feedback of any kind, take it as an opportunity to examine why. Maybe you are an a-hole?

INDUSTRY ETIQUETTE

You can be a great restaurant manager and still not deserve the title "industry." Although the term is applied to various fields, it is associated closely with the hospitality one. You don't see doctors or coal miners lining up at clubs for "industry night."

I carry pride in the name of "industry" to the point where I judge others on whether they are worthy to share the distinction for their own business. Very elitist, I know, but I see it as a badge of honor and entry into a worldwide community that must be earned. The fastest way to determine whether you belong and are worthy of using this terminology is how you conduct yourself in restaurants, both others and your own.

Here are some simple "never" and "always" rules to help you merit the designation "industry."

IN OTHER RESTAURANTS, NEVER...

Never Tell the Staff You Are "Industry:" This boast is akin to someone in your restaurant announcing they are a "foodie." It smacks of entitlement. If you conduct yourself correctly, adept servers and bartenders will recognize that you share the same profession. Announcing your title will have the same effect as giving yourself a nickname—a move that is always viewed as not great. Using it will also be seen as a way to curry a discount, something that you should never do. Speaking of which…

Never Request a Comp: Some restaurants offer industry discounts, and if you know you have arrived on the correct day and time to qualify, then mentioning your affiliation is okay. Otherwise, it is truly an uncool move. Not only does the mention break the rule of announcing to others that you are industry, but it adds a layer of desperation to your request. Keep in mind, restaurant margins are not strong, so the 25 percent+ discount you seek is likely their profit. If someone extends a comp on their own, then they are doing so because they recognize that you are truly "industry" and have enough in their nightly allowance to sacrifice this margin on your behalf. You should always view this gesture as flattering and appreciated but never as expected.

Never Send Back Food: Yes, your food might be prepared incorrectly. It might even be inedible, but sending your food back to the kitchen will likely be perceived as unwarranted. Furthermore, if you are known by members of their team, doing so could reflect negatively on your restaurant. I have consumed frozen ahi tuna, ice chucks and all, rather than insisting on a re-fire. I did so simply because someone on the staff knew who I was. Don't be that person who hassles the kitchen. Seriously, if the food is terrible, order a pizza on your way home.

Never Communicate with a Bouncer: Under no circumstances is chatting with bar security a good idea. It probably means you are attempting to bypass the line, circumvent the dress code, or stop the expulsion of you or a drunk buddy. All are bad ideas. Being a bouncer is not relaxing. You are constantly confronting guests about their behavior, with no clue how they will react.

Working security at a club in Chicago, I was on the receiving end of death threats and sucker punches, simply for asking drunks to leave. I had people spit in my face over my not letting them into the bar. I once tried to break up a fight, only to have them both attempt to choke me out with my tie. Yes, the nightclub made us wear ties, an instant handgrip for combative guests.

Such incidents are common experiences for all bouncers. Most of the time, they're either being challenged for a decision or being persuaded to make an exception. The last thing they need is your arguing dress code in your flip-flops or mentioning that you know the owner. Just don't converse with bouncers. At best, you should learn their names, so you can thank them for standing outside all night to keep you safe.

IN OTHER RESTAURANTS, ALWAYS...

Always Offer a Shot to the Bartender if You Are Buying a Round: Offering the bartender a shot is basic industry courtesy. There are two rules to this practice, though:

Rule #1: You should never buy them a shot in an attempt to hook up. Bartenders get hit on constantly, and although they might reciprocate on occasion, chances are they are not excited about your attempts, especially if your first move is buying a shot. You should extend the offer simply because you are acknowledging the hard work they perform.

Rule #2: You pay for all shots and tip accordingly. Don't think that the bartender doesn't deserve the full tip amount simply because you gave them booze. A shot of Jameson is never a tip.

And please note that they might decline your offer because many restaurants and bars have a policy against staff drinking, but offering is still the respectful thing to do.

Always Split Tabs Equally: Few things are more anti-industry than the request for a server to divide the check eight ways, while requiring them to track exactly what each person consumed. My original rule when dining out was to never split checks under any circumstances.

I trained my non-industry friends to bring cash and throw it in the middle of the table. As people have largely stopped carrying money, the modification is to never divide a bill more than three ways and the division should be equal. If you need to separate it further, work it out among yourselves later.

Do not require the server to spend their time determining who had the spaghetti and who ordered the ribeye for a dozen people. Now, we all have that buddy, the one who protests the even split. "It's not fair that I should pay for Amy's lobster bisque when I only had the local greens," they protest. That person is obnoxious and you should stop inviting them places.

Always Be Mindful of Time: If your server has asked you more than once whether you need anything at the end of your meal, the extra attention is probably because you are their last table. You are likely costing them time that could be used to see their family or nap in-between doubles. If you think you are a server's last table, simply offer to "tab out" so they can close out. The gesture is appreciated and lets them know you are likely in the industry.

Also, it should go without saying that you are never the last table in a restaurant before closing. No matter if they tell you "it's fine," it's not.

Always Tip on the Full Amount: If you are lucky enough to receive a comp, you are obligated to tip on the total before the discount. This practice is a major point in the industry, which an embarrassing number of service people overlook. Keep in mind that those servers and bartenders are still required to tip out their support staff, often on the full amount.

In addition, you must leave more than average. If you did not receive any comps, you should tip no less than 25 percent for service, and this amount is if they spit in your food in front of you. Seriously, 25 percent is minimum, and anyone who says less isn't industry. But if you receive discounts, then you should tip at least 30 percent on the full bill. Not following this rule will no doubt ensure you will pay full price on future visits.

IN YOUR OWN RESTAURANT, NEVER...

Never Call Out Because of a Hangover: Thanks to social media, everyone knows you went out after work. Now you are on the bathroom floor feeling like death. Too bad. Eat a banana and get to work. You did this to yourself. Calling out sick tells everyone you cannot handle your booze, not to mention that someone is required to cover your shift. It's definitely anti-industry.

Never Order During the Rush: If you are lucky enough to work with a restaurant that offers free meals to managers, you need to respect the kitchen. It does not matter if there are zero tickets on the board, ask your chef if it is okay to order before you put in your request. It's basic courtesy. Also, never ask between noon to 1:30 p.m. or between 6:00 p.m. to 9:00 p.m.—ever. Assume they are busy, and you should be on the floor during those times anyway.

Never Trash Other Restaurants: As a manager, hopefully you are taking time to venture to other places. I am assessing facets of every restaurant I visit, hoping to learn a new step of service that I can incorporate in my own venues. These observations would often find their way into pre-shift notes, where I would mention the location and what I found unique and impressive. But if I visited a place and there were terrible missteps in service, I would still discuss in pre-shift, only I never would tell anyone where I went.

This practice is a logical extension of the management rule: "Praise in public; correct in private." The industry is a tight-knit community and your words will find their way back to that venue, guaranteed. Also, it's bad form to trash your competition. You will appear both arrogant in your critical assessment and weak in your petulant complaining. There is a reason no restaurant names appear in this book.

IN YOUR OWN RESTAURANT, ALWAYS...

Always Tip if You Take Up Space: If you decide to take up a seat at the bar or in the restaurant and have your bartender/server wait on you, then you owe them a tip. You are taking up their time. If you are too lazy to walk to the POS and ring in your manager meal yourself, then you should compensate others for doing so. Also, bus your own dishes. Nothing screams inconsiderate more than leaving your dishes for someone else in your restaurant to bus.

Always Know You Come Last: If you visit your own venue during your off hours, whether to dine in or pick up, your order should be placed at the back of the line of tickets. If you are requesting a seat in your restaurant, your party should be seated last and probably in the worst area.

As one of the perks of running your restaurant, you have a comp tab. It comes at the price of making sure the full-paying guests receive the best tables, the quickest service, etc. Think of it like working for an airline. You get to travel free everywhere but you are flying on standby. If they need your seat for a regular passenger, you are waiting for the next plane. When you bring in your friends, they are flying stand-by by proxy. If you wish to be treated like a guest, please pay full fare.

RESOURCES

Here are just a handful of standard restaurant terms to round out your vocabulary:

86ed: Used internally to communicate to staff that a menu item is temporarily unavailable. You would never tell a table, "Sorry folks, but the salmon is 86ed tonight." Apparently, no one can agree on why "86" is used and not 34, 173, or any other random number.

Auctioning: This term applies to instances when a waiter delivers items to a table with the question, "Who had the (blank)?" It is poor service, for sure. If your team utilizes both table and seat numbers properly, there should never be a question regarding who ordered what.

Board: This term refers to the ticket rail used in the kitchen to hold orders in expo. As a restaurant manager, you likely should not leave for the evening until "the board is clear." You definitely should not order your manager meal with a full board.

Clopen: This idiom stems from when someone closes the restaurant one night and is scheduled to open the following morning. Having your staff do clopens is a great way to burn them out and make them leave.

Comp: A slang word for a discount extended to a guest, whether as a courtesy or an attempt to rectify something negative. It is an internal term and should never be used with a guest, like "We are going to comp some desserts for you."

Double/Triple Sat: Optimally, guests are seated in rotation among all servers so one server doesn't get two, three, or more tables in a row. When this situation does occur, being "double sat" or "triple sat" will negatively affect the guest experience. Work to eliminate this possibility from ever happening and offer assistance if it does.

Figure 8: This routine is the path you walk as a manager every 15 minutes, making sure everything is running efficiently. It might include the parking lot, host stand, bar and dining areas, service bar, busser and server stations, kitchen expo, dish station, and all restrooms. It does not include having a smoke next to the dumpster.

In the Weeds: This phrase is used to acknowledge when someone is overwhelmed, often due to a rush—as in: "I was just triple sat. I am definitely in the weeds." It's a common way of asking for help, which you should provide immediately.

On a Count: The phrase means a limited number of a particular item remains available. Most POS systems will allow for inputting this number to let the staff know exactly how many of any item are left before being "86ed." Entering this quantity and communicating it to staff is typically the responsibility of the restaurant manager. For example, by writing, "The salmon is on a four count."

On the Floor: The floor is the guest dining space. It is used internally such as in: "Manager Amy spends too much time in the office. She should be on the floor more."

On the Fly: This phrase is used when an item needs to be prepared immediately. The reasons usually are server/bartender forgot to ring it in, kitchen missed it on the ticket, or guest did not like the original offering. All of these instances require you to table touch and gauge the guest's level of disappointment.

Postmortem: In medicine, this procedure is the examination of a dead body. In hospitality, the meaning denotes a post-shift to examine how the evening went. Based on the morbid nature of the term, these reviews have a tendency to be requested after particular turbulent services.

Truck-Stop Bussing: This practice refers to clearing multiple drinks simultaneously by inserting one's fingers inside the glass and carrying them like a bowling ball. It is super gross.

ACKNOWLEDGEMENTS

The Surprise Restaurant Manager: Published by Korgen Hospitality

SPECIAL THANKS GOES TO:

Fabio Viviani for the amazing foreword, though I will point out I am eating less McDonald's these days.

Michelle Winkley from Talent Distinctions. She was my resource for all HR aspects and generally keeps me grounded.

Lance French for teaching me the Four Essential Words. I use them as often as possible.

Sarah Zelman for the great author photography. I wish I looked that good in real life.

And my mom, **Carole McGarrie**. Thank you for all the editing advice long before this book got to the publishers and for continuing to encourage me to write, even when it looked like I never would.

ENDNOTES

1   Shamsian, Jacob. "The Common Statistic That 'Half of Marriages End in Divorce' Is Bogus." Insider. Insider, February 9, 2017. https://www.insider.com/what-is-the-divorce-rate-2017-2.

2   Yau, Nathan. "Divorce and Occupation." FlowingData, November 18, 2019. https://flowingdata.com/2017/07/25/divorce-and-occupation.

3   Bush, Donna M., and Rachel N. Lipari. "SUBSTANCE USE AND SUBSTANCE USE DISORDER BY INDUSTRY." Substance Use and Substance Use Disorder by Industry. The Substance Abuse and Mental Health Services Administration (SAMHSA), 2012. https://www.samhsa.gov/data/sites/default/files/report_1959/ShortReport-1959.html.

4   "Drug Addiction (Substance Use Disorder)." Mayo Clinic. Mayo Foundation for Medical Education and Research, October 26, 2017. https://www.mayoclinic.org/diseases-conditions/drug-addiction/symptoms-causes/syc-20365112.

5   Han, Beth, Alex E Crosby, LaVonne A G Ortega, Sharyn E Parks, Wilson M Compton, and Joseph Gfroerer. "Suicidal Ideation, Suicide Attempt, and Occupations among Employed Adults Aged 18-64years in the United States." Comprehensive psychiatry. U.S. National Library of Medicine, April 2016. https://www.ncbi.nlm.nih.gov/pmc/articles/PMC4959536/.

6   Bruner, Jerome. "Discovery Learning ." Learning Theories, March 5, 2020. https://www.learning-theories.com/discovery-learning-bruner.html.

Printed in Great Britain
by Amazon